TRACING

$\mathcal{S}$ COTTISH ANCESTORS

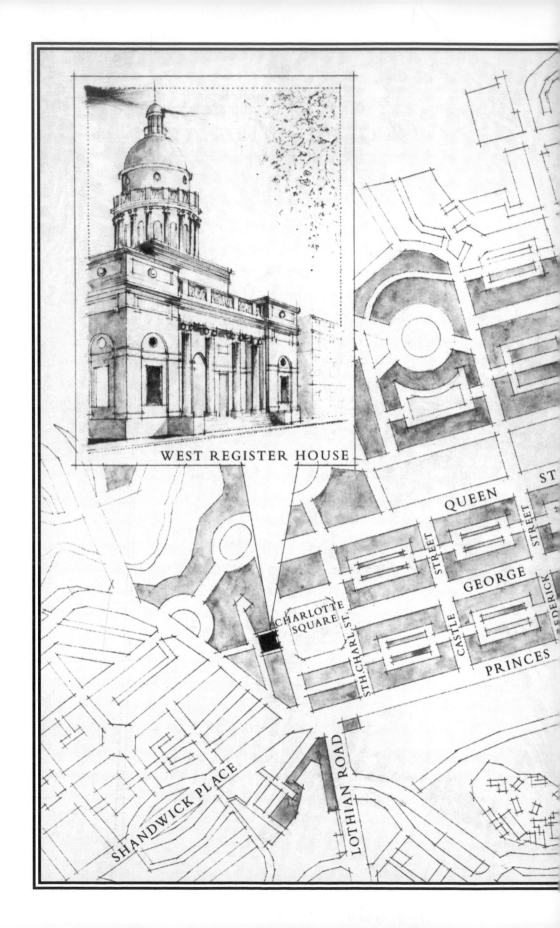

WEST REGISTER HOUSE

QUEEN

STREET

QUEEN STREET

GEORGE STREET

PRINCES

CHARLOTTE SQUARE

CASTLE STREET

STH.CHARL. ST.

FREDERICK

SHANDWICK PLACE

LOTHIAN ROAD

$\mathcal{H}$OW TO GET THERE

GENERAL REGISTER HOUSE

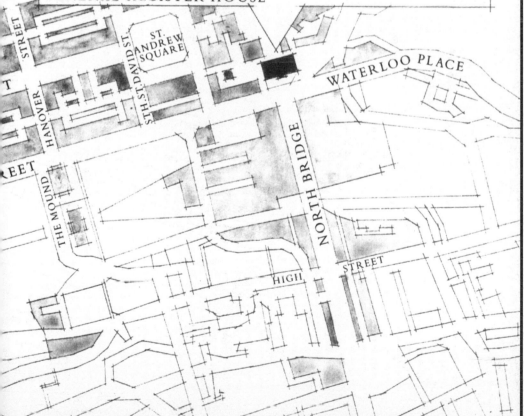

General Register House

TRACING YOUR

Scottish Ancestors

A GUIDE TO
ANCESTRY RESEARCH
IN THE
SCOTTISH RECORD OFFICE

Revised Edition

Cecil Sinclair

EDINBURGH: THE STATIONERY OFFICE

Revised edition published 1997 by
The Stationery Office Limited
South Gyle Crescent, Edinburgh EH12 9EB

Applications for reproduction should be made to the Crown Copyright Unit
St Clements House, 1–16 Colegate, Norwich NR3 1BQ

British Library Cataloguing in Publication Data

A catalogue record of this book is available from the British Library

Cover photograph by Creative Photography

ISBN 0 11 495865 3

Author's Note

In writing this Guide, I have been much indebted to the advice and suggestions which I have received from my curatorial colleagues. The responsibility for the wording and content of the text and any errors and omissions is, however, entirely mine.

CECIL SINCLAIR

$\mathcal{C}$ontents

$\mathscr{P}$reface to the First Edition

HM General Register House, Edinburgh, has been the home of the Public Records of Scotland for over 200 years. In 1847 certain classes of records were open to the public free of charge for approved, historical antiquarian and literary searchers. Since then it has been recognised as one of the main centres for Scottish genealogical research and family history enquiries have formed an ever-growing part of its business.

In his pioneering guide to Scottish genealogical research, *The Pursuit of Pedigree* (1928), Hector M'Kechnie (1899-1966) wrote that the staff of the Historical Department 'seem able to cope with the constant fire of interruption to which they are subjected by students who cannot find the right source for their purpose, cannot read it when it has been found, or cannot understand it when read'. Dealing with a relatively small number of readers, they were able to make up for the lack of guides and indexes by a degree of individual attention which would be impossible in today's conditions.

When Mr Sinclair and I joined the staff in the early 1950s the Historical Search Room was certainly busier than it had been in 1928, but the general picture given by M'Kechnie had not altered noticeably. Since then changes have been deep and far-reaching. The Scottish Record Office's holdings have almost trebled and are now spread over two main buildings and two smaller record stores. The number of readers has increased ten-fold, with an even greater proportional increase in genealogical enquirers. This changed situation has led to a changed approach, with greater emphasis on self-help through the provision of more and better findings aids. I hope, however, that the helpfulness of staff is still as evident to today's visitors as it was sixty years ago.

This *Guide* is an extension of the idea of self-help, to enable family historians to assess likely sources of information before they come to the SRO and make the best use of their time once they are there. It may seem strange that they are advised to go to another department first, but the statutory registers of births, marriages and deaths, the census records and the old parochial registers held by the General Register Office (Scotland) in New Register House form the most logical starting point for the family historian. I am grateful to my colleague, Dr John Shaw, formerly Departmental Record Officer at GRO(S), for contributing the chapter on its record holdings and to Dr Charles M Glennie, Registrar General for Scotland, for his kind agreement that it should appear in this volume.

In recent years there have been a number of publications wholly or partly concerned with genealogical research in Scotland. Some of the best have been written by professional genealogists from the knowledge and experience which they have gained as users of the records. Mr Sinclair writes from a different perspective, that of a custodian of records, with insights acquired through handling them over many years. He has also been able to draw on the knowledge and experience of colleagues, who have had the opportunity of getting to know the records themselves and the varying needs of users. For my own part, I doubt whether any author or genealogist, looking as it were from the outside, can ever match an insider's depth and width of knowledge of the records.

However good the guidance provided by reference books such as this, the success of the family historian's work will ultimately depend on his own ability to identify and understand the information which the records contain. As Hector M'Kechnie put it: 'In short, one has to face trials and troubles of both a treasure-hunt and a jig-saw puzzle'. But, as with a treasure-hunt and a jigsaw puzzle, there can be great satisfaction in working out the clues and arriving at the correct solution.

ATHOL MURRAY
Keeper of the Records of Scotland

Preface to the Revised Edition

Mr Sinclair's book has been an outstanding success. Widely purchased and consulted, and of the greatest value to family historians of all levels of competence, it has also been extremely useful to the staff of the Scottish Record Office. It is, as Dr Murray says, 'an extension of the idea of self help', and I believe that it is for this reason that it has been so much appreciated by all those who have used it.

This revised edition is therefore to be welcomed. It contains some minor alterations throughout the text, and the chapter on the General Register Office for Scotland has been substantially rewritten to take account of developments since 1990. I would like to thank Bruno Longmore for rewriting the chapter and Mr James Meldrum, Registrar General for Scotland, for his permission to include it in this new edition. Otherwise, the format which has proved so useful has been preserved. I am sure that *Tracing Your Scottish Ancestors* will continue to be as popular and useful as it has been over the last seven years.

PATRICK CADELL
Keeper of the Records of Scotland

$\mathcal{I}$ntroduction

They trace his steps till they can tell
His pedigree as weel's himsell
Robert Fergusson

1.1 You want to find your Scottish ancestors. This book is written specifically to help you to trace those ancestors who are mentioned in the documents preserved in the Scottish Record Office, a primary location of records for family research.

Legacy in will, 1710. (CC.20/4/17)

The Scottish Record Office

1.2 The Scottish Record Office is the government department responsible for the custody and preservation of the records of the government of Scotland. It also has taken responsibility for and custody of the records of many non-government concerns, including church records and the records of some private families and businesses. Most of these records may be consulted by members of the public.

1.3 The Scottish Record Office occupies two buildings in the centre of Edinburgh, close to the railway and bus stations. One building is General Register House, at the east end of Princes Street, opposite the Balmoral (better known as the North British) Hotel and the General Post Office. A statue of the Duke of Wellington ('the man on the horse') guards the entrance to this building, which houses, as well as many records, two search rooms, the Legal Search Room and the Historical Search Room. As searching for your ancestors is regarded as historical research, you will use the Historical Search Room. If you want to see any of the records for a legal purpose, then you will use the Legal Search Room and be charged a fee. You will not be charged for doing historical research, but you must do your own research. The staff will advise you and try to answer all reasonable questions, but the rest is up to you. Hence this book!

1.4 The second building, West Register House, is situated in Charlotte Square, about a mile away from General Register House. It also contains a search room, the West Search Room, in which you may do historical research. The same rules, regulations and procedures apply to both Historical and West Search Rooms. Both are open from Monday to Friday, 09.00 - 16.45 hours, apart from certain public holidays and a period of annual stocktaking in November.

1.5 Confusingly, there is another building called New Register House, which is adjacent to General Register House but is not part of the Scottish Record Office. This building houses the General Register Office for Scotland and the official records of births, marriages and deaths and census records. Because of the paramount importance of these records to the family historian, they are described in Chapter 3, although not directly within the bounds of this book.

About this Book

1.6 The first four chapters are introductory ones, which you should read before planning a visit to or writing to the Scottish Record Office. Chapters 5-28 describe records in the Scottish Record Office which might be of use to you in your search for your ancestors. In a sense, all records which name individuals may provide genealogical information, but the author has tried to select and describe those which will be most useful. Chapters 5-10 concern records which should be of interest to all ancestor hunters: records of baptism, marriage, death, inheritance, land-owning and tenancy. The remaining chapters describe records which concern particular activities or professions or situations, records which are less likely to specify relationships, though they may, but will add foliage to your family tree.

1.7 An attempt has been made to lead the reader step-by-step into the records, particularly those records described in the earlier chapters which should prove the most profitable. The intention is to enable you to do your research with decreasing reliance on the advice of the staff. Descriptions of procedures in the later pages of the book will assume that you have become familiar with the techniques of searching records.

1.8 As this book is intended specifically to help genealogical researchers, it does not cover all the records in the Scottish Record Office or deal with all aspects of the records which are described. Legal concepts may be simplified in their description.

1.9 While reading this book, you will encounter unfamiliar words, not all of which are explained. There will also be unfamiliar words in the records which you are going to search. Get into the habit of using a dictionary, such as *The Concise Scots Dictionary* (Aberdeen University Press).

1.10 Most of the published works to which the reader is referred in the course of this book should be available in the United Kingdom through a local library, perhaps by inter-library loan. The names of publishers are placed in brackets after the titles of recently-published books, but not out-of-print ones.

1.11 In his use of personal pronouns, the author has described your ancestors as if they were all male. This is a matter of convenience and the author apologises to those who are rightly offended. However, it is a fact that men are more likely to be named in the records than women.

1.12 Throughout the rest of this book, the Scottish Record Office will be represented by the initials SRO. All paragraphs in the book are numbered and a reference to a paragraph from elsewhere in the book will be by its number. A reference to this paragraph would be simply 1.12.

Postal Enquiries

1.13 While this book is primarily designed to help people to do their own research in the SRO, the author hopes that it will also help and guide those who are unable to come to Edinburgh, but who wish to trace their Scottish ancestry. Unfortunately, while postal enquiries are welcome, the staff of the SRO, because of pressure of work, cannot do extended research on behalf of enquirers. Staff will provide advice and will answer very limited and specific enquiries, such as for the will of a named person whose locality and approximate date of death are provided. Accordingly, if you require extended research to be done for you, you should consider employing a professional searcher. A list of those currently working in Scotland will be sent on request.

1.14 Please do not send any financial remittance unless and until you are requested to do so.

1.15 All correspondence should be addressed to

The Keeper of the Records of Scotland
Scottish Record Office
H M General Register House
Edinburgh EH1 3YY
Scotland

The telephone number is a 0131-535 1314 and the fax number is 0131-535 1360.

$\mathcal{F}$irst Steps in Family Research

2.1 The Scottish Record Office will not be your first port of call when you decide to find out who your ancestors were. First ask your Aunt Jessie. In other words, you begin with your own living family. There is usually at least one elderly relative who is interested in the family and acts as the family memory, though that memory may be reliable for only a couple of generations back. (Be wary of romantic family traditions that claim descent from the disinherited child of a nobleman or from the owner of a castle.) Some of your relatives may have preserved old family letters and documents such as birth certificates and wills. Also, if the family has lived in the same locality for some generations, it will be worth looking at gravestones in the local kirkyard or graveyard.

Wedding photograph, 1890. (Private family collection)

2.2 From this information, you will have a basis on which to build. If you live in
Scotland, your next step is to visit your local library. Even if you live in another
country, your local library may be able to obtain useful books for you. If your
ancestors stayed for a long time in one area, familiarise yourself with that area,
by means of studying local maps, e.g. Victorian large-scale Ordnance Survey
maps, reading parish histories, checking if the local library has any street
directories.

2.3 If your ancestor was genuinely a product of a noble or landed family, you
should look at *The Scots Peerage* or *Burke's Peerage, Baronetage and Knightage* or
Burke's Landed Gentry. Useful guides to printed sources on particular families
are *Scottish Family History* by Margaret Stuart and Balfour Paul and *Scottish
Family Histories* by J P S Ferguson (National Library of Scotland). Miss
Ferguson has also produced a *Directory of Scottish Newspapers* (National Library
of Scotland), which will tell you which Scottish libraries hold copies of a
particular local newspaper. If an ancestor was a local dignitary, there may be an
obituary of him in a local newspaper. The annual volumes of the *Edinburgh
Almanack* name office holders throughout Scotland since the mid-18th
century.

2.4 To find out information about an ancestor, you must know in what part of
Scotland he lived. You must also have some knowledge of the administrative
areas into which Scotland was divided. The present division into regions and
districts dates only from 1975. For centuries, the basic units were the parish,
burgh, county and sheriffdom, and you should try to find out in which of these
your ancestors may have lived. The General Register Office has produced a
useful *Index of Scottish Place Names from 1971 Census* (The Stationery Office),
which lists the then inhabited places in Scotland, showing the county and
parish in which each was located. If this publication is not available or you
cannot find a place-name in it, try a pre-1975 gazetteer or a 19th century
edition of the *County Directory of Scotland*, which gives the nearest town and
sometimes the county of inhabited places. A useful index of parishes, showing
the related counties, sheriffdoms, commissary courts (see chapter 6) and burghs
is obtainable from Mrs A R Bigwood, 38 Primrose Bank Road, Edinburgh
EH5 3JF, who has compiled it. Another alphabetical list of parishes, showing the
sheriffdom, diocese, presbytery and commissariot of each is printed in *An
Historical Catalogue of the Scottish Bishops* by Robert Keith (published in 1824)
and in *In Search of Scottish Ancestry* by Gerald Hamilton-Edwards (Phillimore).
As the boundaries of parishes and other administrative areas did not remain the
same throughout the centuries and human beings are often mobile, you should
note the names of adjacent parishes and other areas in case you need to extend
your search to them. There was a particularly significant alteration of county
and parish boundaries in 1891.

2.5 If you want to find out about the history of your surname (as opposed to that
of your family), look it up in *The Surnames of Scotland* by George F Black
(New York Public Library). However, names can be a snare sometimes, as it is
only in comparatively recent times that we have spelled names consistently.

An ancestor may have had the same surname as you but spelled it differently. Clerks writing this surname down in official documents might spell it in yet other ways. Even with Christian names, you have to be canny: e.g. Patrick and Peter used to be interchangeable names. But with Christian names, you have the marvellous advantage in the admirable practice of naming almost every child after a relative. Thus, it is reasonable to expect that an eldest son is named after his father's father, the second after his mother's father, the third after his own father, an eldest daughter after her mother's mother, the second after her father's mother, and the third after her own mother, and younger children after available uncles and aunts. A practice less convenient for us, however, was the naming of infants after elder brothers and sisters who had died: another snare for the genealogist.

2.6 Your preliminary investigation complete, you are ready to look at original documents in a record office. Before starting your research in the SRO, you should first go to the General Register Office to look at the records of births, deaths and marriages and census records. These are described in Chapter 3.

3

The General Register Office for Scotland
(The Registrar-General's Department)
by Bruno B W Longmore

3.1 Under the direction of the Registrar General for Scotland, the General Register Office for Scotland (GRO(S)), a Government department, administers the registration of births, deaths and marriages. The Registrar General is also responsible for the taking of periodic decennial censuses of the population of Scotland. The GRO(S) is located in New Register House in Edinburgh, conveniently situated for family historians, next door to the SRO's main building, General Register House.

3.2 For people interested in doing their family history, various leaflets are available from the GRO(S) and are updated each year: *A List of the Main Records in the Care of the Registrar General*; *Searching by Our Staff for a Particular Event*; and *Guidance for General Search Customers in New Register House*. You can obtain copies by calling in person or writing, faxing or telephoning New Register House, Edinburgh EH1 3YT (telephone: 0131-334 0380; fax: 0131-314 4400; international code +44 131). Full texts of the leaflets, and further information about GRO(S), are on the World Wide Web at:
http://www/open.gov.uk/gros/groshome.htm.

3.3 Through the same telephone numbers (or 0131-314 4449 or 4450) you may reserve one of the limited number of search-room seats for advance booking, or make use of a discounted advance-purchase pass (Apex) when available. While it is not necessary to book in advance, you are advised to do so if travelling any distance to Edinburgh, as there is a great demand for seats, particularly during the summer months. A place booked for a particular day will be held for you *until 10:00*, but if you fail to appear or do not call to say that you have been delayed, the place may be let to someone else. Alternatively, you can simply come to New Register House without a booking, as many of our search places are filled on a 'first-come, first-served' basis.

3.4 Booking a place is free, but you will need to buy a valid pass to search the records. You can buy a search pass for a day; a week; four weeks; a quarter or a year. A part-day search pass is also available, but only after 13:00, and no advance bookings for part-day searches can be made. Paying the statutory fee for a search pass gives you the right to search in the indexes to the post-1855 statutory registers of births, deaths and marriages; the pre-1855 old parish registers (OPRs); and the open census returns 1841 to 1891. You also have a right to buy an extract that is, an authenticated copy of any individual register entry.

3.5 In addition, at the discretion of the Registrar General, those who have paid the fee are also permitted to look at microfiche or microfilm copies of the actual entries in the registers of births, deaths and marriages etc. identified from the indexes, and to take notes. For statutory register entries over 100 years old, you can also buy unauthenticated photocopies.

3.6 New Register House is open Mondays to Fridays (except public holidays) between the hours of 09:00 and 16:30. Access to the records is not allowed to anyone under the age of 12. Children of 12 or 13 may be allowed access only if accompanied by their parent or legal guardian. Children aged 14 to 16 may be allowed access unaccompanied provided they can show written parental or guardian consent to their searching the records. Normal fees are payable in all cases. Tell the staff in advance if you have any disability which might make it difficult for you to use the search facilities. A search in the GRO(S) involves, for example, moving around the building, opening filing-cabinet drawers of various heights, and viewing a computer screen and microfiche reader. If you have difficulty doing this, free admission may be given to someone assisting you.

3.7 On arrival you will be issued with a numbered ticket and directed through to a waiting-room. If you have already paid in advance for an Apex pass, ask as you come in and you can collect it without waiting. When it is your turn to be served your number will be displayed, and you should go through to the nearby public counter where the staff will discuss with you the kind of search you wish to do, and ask you for the appropriate fee. They will issue you with a search pass and a seat number, and direct you to the appropriate search room where your numbered seat is located. There are four search rooms in New Register House with a total of just over 100 search places. The pass for New Register House is personal and not normally transferable to anyone else, though special rules apply to one-year passes.

3.8 The supervisor in the search room will give you a short introduction on how to use the facilities and how to order out the records. Your searching will involve computer indexes; microfiche and microfilm readers; the location of the fiche and film; and of the finding aids and reference books, which are easy to use.

3.9 Records in New Register House are available by means of self-service access on microfiche or microfilm. You can withdraw a fiche or film from the self-service areas by completing the appropriate order-slip. Insert the completed order-slip in place of the fiche or film you wish to look at, and take it back to the reader equipment located on your desk. You can take out up to three microfiche or two microfilm reels at any one time. When you have finished with any record, you simply leave it in the appropriate tray for re-filing by the staff. Search-room staff are available to give guidance, but not to conduct searches for you.

3.10 To protect the valuable records, you will only be allowed to use a pencil, not a pen, when taking your own notes, and you will not be permitted to smoke, eat or drink anywhere in New Register House, including the toilet areas. There are many cafes, pubs, restaurants and sandwich-bars within easy walking distance.

Births, Deaths and Marriages since 1855

3.11 In Scotland compulsory civil registration of births, deaths and marriages commenced on 1 January 1855 under the Registration of Births, Deaths and Marriages (Scotland) Act 1854. Tracing a line of descent back to 1855 can be a fairly straightforward task provided you start with some good details about more recent members of your family. The GRO(S) holds a complete set of the statutory registers comprising all the births, deaths and marriages registered since 1855 in all the registration districts in Scotland, originally 1027 in number. It is likely that you will want to start your family search in these registers, unless your ancestors left Scotland before 1855.

3.12 Within a few weeks of any birth, death or marriage being registered in Scotland, the event is added to the appropriate computer index, and simple step-by-step instructions are provided for working the easy-to-use computer terminals in the search rooms. All events registered since 1855 can now be looked up on the computer, but the computer indexes were in the main prepared from paper indexes compiled at the time, so their contents vary.

3.13 The *birth indexes* give details of the child's name; the year of registration; registration district name and number; and register entry number. From 1929 onwards the mother's maiden surname is also given.

3.14 The *death indexes* give the deceased's name; age at death; the year of registration; registration district name and number; and register entry number. From 1855 to 1865 the age at death was not recorded in the old paper indexes, but these ages are gradually being added to the computer indexes. Separate entries exist for both female married names and maiden names. From 1974, the mother's surname is included for both male and female deaths. Ages given by informants may be only approximate, particularly in the early decades of registration, and in the cases of persons born before compulsory civil registration began.

3.15 The *marriage indexes* give each party's name; the year of registration; registration district name and number; and register entry number. From 1929 onwards, the spouse's surname is also given.

3.16 There are a number of points to note about the indexes. First, the spelling of names may be unusual, particularly during the earlier period of registration.

The indexes record the names as spelt by the registrar at the time, irrespective of present-day spelling. To help overcome these variations, a Soundex facility has been incorporated into the indexes, and this can be used to identify alternative spellings or similar sounding surnames. Secondly, names beginning 'Mac' and 'Mc' are indexed separately. You should therefore check both if you have difficulty in finding the entry you are looking for. Once you have traced an entry you would like to see in the indexes, consult the register entry itself.

3.17 Entries in the statutory registers of births from 1861 include: name, date, time and place of birth; sex; father's name and profession; mother's name and maiden name; date and place of marriage; signature and qualification of informant, and residence if out of the house in which the birth occurred.

3.18 Entries in the registers of deaths from 1861 include: name; rank or profession; marital status; spouse's name; when and where died; sex; age; father's name and rank or profession; mother's name and maiden name; cause of death; signature and qualification of informant, and residence if out of the house in which the death occurred.

3.19 Entries in the register of marriages from 1861 include: when, where and how married (e.g. after banns, according to the forms of the Church of Scotland). For both bridegroom and bride are given: name; rank or profession; marital status; age; usual residence; father's name and rank or profession; mother's name and maiden name. In the case of regular marriages, names of the officiating minister (or registrar from 1940) and witnesses are recorded. In the case of irregular marriages, date of conviction (to 1939), decree of declarator, or sheriff's warrant is given.

3.20 You will find that there is some variation from the above in the information registered between 1855 and 1860. The first year of civil registration in Scotland, 1855, is particularly good, with fuller details recorded about individuals and their families. If you are lucky enough to find an ancestor who was born, died or married in this year, the additional information supplied can be very full indeed and may include some of the following details.

- *in the registers of births for 1855:* name; whether informant present at birth; baptismal name (if different) or name given without baptism; sex; date, and time of birth; where born; father's name and rank, profession or occupation, age and birthplace; when and where married, and any previous issue, both living and deceased; mother's name and maiden name, how many children she has had, age and where born; signature and qualification of informant, and residence if out of the house where the birth occurred.

- *in the registers of deaths for 1855:* name; rank, profession or occupation; sex; age; where born and how long in district; parents' names, and rank, profession or occupation; if married, spouse's name and names and ages of any children; date of death and time; where died; cause of death, length of illness, by whom certified and when they last saw the deceased; burial place, undertaker by whom certified; signature and qualification of informant.

- *in the registers of marriages for 1855:* when, where and how married; (and, for both bridegroom and bride) signatures; present and usual residences; age; rank and profession; relationship of parties, if related; marital status; children by any previous marriages, whether living or dead; where parties were born; the date and place of registration of birth; parents' names, rank, profession or occupation; if a regular marriage, signatures of officiating minister and witnesses; if irregular, date of conviction or decree of declarator and court pronounced.

3.21 There are also minor variations from 1966 to 1995 and from 1996.

3.22 Corrections or changes to the registered particulars–for example, in the cases of divorce or change of name–are recorded in the *Register of Corrected Entries*, or *Register of Corrections Etc.* The entries in the registers of births, deaths and marriages are cross-referenced to these.

3.23 The GRO(S) also holds indexes for series of records of births, deaths and marriages which occurred outside Scotland, but which relate to Scots:

- Marine register of births and deaths (from 1855);
- Air register of births and deaths (from 1948);
- Service records (from 1881);
- War registers (from 1899);
- Consular returns of births, deaths and marriages (from 1914);
- High Commissioners' returns of births and deaths (from 1964);
- Registers of births, deaths and marriages in foreign countries (1860-1965);
- Foreign marriages (from 1947).

These records are in some cases patchy and incomplete. Further details about them are in the GRO(S) leaflet, *List of main records in the care of the Registrar General*.

3.24 The statutory registers of births, deaths and marriages are all duplicated, with one copy held centrally in New Register House, as described, and a second copy held locally. While there is limited provision for searching the duplicate copies held by local registrars, a number of local search centres now exist which contain copies of fiche for areas other than their own strict registration area. Some offices have on-line access to the computerised indexes at New Register House. Before you visit a local registration office it is advisable to telephone first to ask about their facilities.

Births, Deaths and Marriages before 1855

3.25 If you have been lucky enough to get back beyond the year 1855, and have not come to a dead end during your search of the Scottish statutory registers–which may happen if, for example, your ancestors came to Scotland from Ireland–then the old parish registers (OPRs) may take you further back beyond this date. Many of these registers are available in the GRO(S), where those that survived were deposited under the Registration Act of 1854 to form a splendid continuity with the statutory registers.

3.26 The OPRs are the registers of the established Church, the Church of Scotland, which record births and baptisms; proclamations of banns or marriages; and deaths or burials, up to 1854. The parish ministers or session clerks of some 900 parishes kept these registers until their formal transfer to the GRO(S). The surviving registers number approximately 3,500 but they are far from complete. Though the oldest register relates to baptisms and banns in 1553 for the parish of Errol in Perthshire, for some parishes the earliest registers date from the early 19th century, while for others there may be no registers at all. A lot of parishes do not have any burial or death registers. The standard of record-keeping varied considerably from parish to parish and from year to year, and most entries contain relatively little information in comparison to the statutory registers.

3.27 You should therefore set out with optimism tinged with realism when tackling the OPRs. Remember also that although registration in the Church of Scotland's registers was in theory compulsory for all denominations, it was both costly and unpopular. Members of other churches, such as the Free Church of Scotland or Roman Catholic Church, may not be recorded, though with luck you may be able to find some (see chapter 5 for alternatives). Also, as populations shifted and cities started to develop in the 19th century, religion began to lose its hold, and as few as 30 per cent of events may be recorded for certain urban parishes.

3.28 There are computer indexes to all the registers of births and baptisms, and of banns and marriages. There are no computer indexes for the registers of deaths or burials, but paper indexes exist for a few of them. Lists of the indexed material are available in each of the search rooms. The OPRs have been added to the Genealogical Society of Utah's *International Genealogical Index* (IGI) and to its *FamilySearch* family-history software, which is also available for reference in New Register House.

3.29 The OPR computerised indexes contain some seven million birth, baptism and marriage entries. You can search either the whole of Scotland for a particular name, or just a specific county and decade, for example Perthshire for 1800-1809.

3.30 The *births and baptism indexes* give details of the child's name; parents' names; date of birth or baptism; and the reference number and name of the parish where the baptism took place.

3.31 The *banns and marriages indexes* give the name of the person who was married; the name of their spouse; date of proclamation or marriage; and the reference number and name of the parish where the marriage took place.

3.32 The GRO(S) has a catalogue of the OPRs arranged alphabetically by parish name within counties. This gives details of the dates covered for each type of event, and the reference numbers allocated to each register. If you have the name of a place but do not know what parish it is in, there is a collection of directories, gazetteers and maps in the New Register House Library to assist you. To preserve the original OPR volumes from overuse, consultation of the registers is from microfilm alone.

3.33 There are no hard and fast rules about the details given in the OPR pages themselves. These vary from parish to parish, and the information can be very thin. In the case of baptisms, aside from the name of the child and the date of the baptism, you might hope to obtain the names of both parents, their place or parish of residence, and perhaps the occupation of the father. On some occasions a list of witnesses may be supplied. For marriages, you might expect to find the date on which the marriage took place or was contracted, the names of the parties and their place or parishes of residence. If you are lucky enough to have an ancestor with a relatively uncommon surname, this can be useful when attempting to identify the correct entry from the indexes. Unfortunately, remote parishes such as those in the Highlands are notoriously difficult, with the same combinations of Christian names and surnames common to particular localities. These names may crop up again and again, for example, John Mackay; Kenneth Mackenzie; Mary Macdonald; Ann Ross; Margaret Fraser.

Census Records (1841-1891)

3.34 Census records can make an excellent bonus for the family historian who visits New Register House. They can both fill out information about families already traced in the registers of births, deaths and marriages and other sources, and lead you to ancestors or family members whom you had not previously identified.

3.35 The Registrar General holds records of the decennial census of the population of Scotland for 1841 and every tenth year thereafter (with the exception of the wartime year of 1941 when no census was taken). The records of censuses taken after 1891 are still confidential and are not available for searching or extracting until 100 years after the date of each census. The only records open for the public to see relate to the censuses held on 7 June 1841; 31 March 1851; 8 April 1861; 3 April 1871; 4 April 1881 and 5 April 1891. These records are transcript books prepared by the census enumerators after the census schedules were collected from individual households within each parish.

3.36 The census books generally contain particulars such as name; age; sex; marital status; relationship to head of the household; occupation and birthplace of every member of a household present at that address on census night, including servants, lodgers and visitors. However, details do vary from census year to census year.

3.37 The returns for the 1841 census year are the least detailed. Marital status and relationship to head of the household was not recorded. Birthplace details confirm only if an individual was born within the Scottish county being enumerated or not. If the person was born outwith that county, unfortunately no other county name is given and, if born furth of Scotland, only the initial letter of the country of birth is given: for example, 'E' for England; 'I' for Ireland; 'F' for France. Also, the ages given may not always be accurate. In some cases enumerators may have recorded the actual age given, but they were instructed to round down ages for persons over the age of 15. Thus, persons between the ages of 15 and 20 can have age recorded as 15; between 20 and 25 recorded as 20; between 25 and 30 recorded as 25, etc.

3.38 By the year 1851, marital status; relationship to head of the household; and fuller details of birthplace, including place and county of birth were added. Details of whether a person was blind or deaf and dumb are also noted By 1861, additional details such as number of children attending school; and numbers of rooms with one or more windows are also recorded. These will help you to build a more detailed picture of your ancestors, their family circumstances, and the accommodation in which they lived.

3.39 The entries in the census books were not indexed by the enumerators, and in order to trace any particular family one needs to have some knowledge of the address they were at when the census was taken. Street indexes are available for certain large urban areas and the bigger towns. These identify the census books for each small 'enumeration district' in which addresses are recorded, and are invaluable particularly for the cities, which cover many books. At the front of each enumeration book you will find a short description of the area it covers. Add to this the difficulty of different parts of streets often being included in several enumeration districts, and the tedium of looking through, for example, the city of Glasgow census returns without street indexes can be imagined. When searching census records, therefore, you should start out with enough information to identify positively the person or family you are looking for, including their town or parish of residence. For people living in large towns, it greatly helps to know their exact address.

3.40 The GRO(S) holds catalogues from which you can identify the census districts and the reference numbers for these. For the census years 1841 and 1851, the districts are arranged alphabetically within counties. For later censuses they are simply arranged alphabetically.

3.41 The GRO(S) has also made available two computerised indexes of all the names enumerated for the census years 1881 and 1891. They consist of over three million entries for each census year and will permit you to search these records more easily.

3.42 The 1881 census index consists of a full set of all the information contained in the enumerators' transcript books. You can search this index and discover complete details of the enumerated entries for each household, and the specific details for each individual within that household. In theory, therefore, it is not necessary to inspect the original census record, though we would always recommend that you do so in order to satisfy yourself that you have obtained the correct census information.

3.43 The 1891 census index consists of index entries only, similar to the indexes for the statutory registers and OPRs. The 1891 index gives details of name; sex; age; name and number of the registration district and enumeration district; and page number of the census entry. It will always be necessary to inspect the original 1891 census record on microfilm.

3.44 In addition to these indexes, certain privately produced indexes for other census years and specific counties or parishes are available and these are continually being added to. They are far from being a complete coverage of all the census data, but they may be of possible use if your ancestors came from particular areas. Details of these are available in the search rooms.

3.45 As with the old parish registers, consultation of the census records is from microfilm alone. Copies of these and the OPR microfilms are sold to libraries and other institutions throughout the world. It is therefore possible to inspect many of these films in places other than the GRO(S). Access to the computer indexes, on the other hand, is available only at New Register House and a few registration offices in Scotland.

4

At the Scottish Record Office

4.1 You are now ready to visit the Scottish Record Office. Try to be clear in your mind what information you are seeking and what records you want to see. Before your first visit, especially if you do not live in Edinburgh, you should write to the Keeper of the Records of Scotland to find out where the records you want to see may be consulted. Records may be in General Register House or West Register House or in a local record office elsewhere in Scotland (see Appendix A). Some records are stored in buildings in the suburbs of Edinburgh and consequently a few days notice will be required before you can see such records in a search room. As records are sometimes transferred from one location to another, the present location of most of the records is not specified in this book. However, you will probably go first to General Register House, as the records currently held there include the legal registers, executry records and church records. Please also give advance notice if you are disabled or if you want to use your tape-recorder, typewriter or personal computer. Facilities for the use of such equipment are very limited. Seats in the Search Rooms are not bookable in advance.

4.2 When you arrive at the front door of General (or West) Register House, tell the duty staff that you have come to do research in the Historical (or West) Search Room, and they will direct you there. On your first visit, you will have to complete a visitor's form. Thereafter, show your reader's ticket to gain admittance. Remember to bring a pencil with you every time, as ink in any form is banned from the search rooms (in case of accidental damage to the records). Bring notepaper. On your first visit, bring a means of identification. Do not leave these essentials in the cloakroom or locker where you must leave your outer garments and bag.

4.3 You have climbed the stairs to one of the search rooms on your first visit to the SRO. A member of staff will interview you, issue you with a reader's ticket and a copy of the search room regulations, show you where the catalogues and indexes are kept, and give such preliminary advice as is required. Your reader's ticket will be valid for up to three years. Keep it carefully, as it entitles you to see the records free-of-charge. You will be asked to hand it over every time you order out any records.

4.4 Though staff are at hand to advise you further and to answer reasonable questions, you are the one who is going to research the records. The records are divided into various groups, listed in a Summary Catalogue of all the records. Each record group has its own reference code, consisting of letters (eg AD, CC, E, GD). Each document has its own unique reference (or call) number, consisting of a group code followed by a series of numbers (eg AD.14/53/203). The guides to the records take various forms and some are easier to use or more thorough than others. Each group of records has its own catalogue, either a repertory or an inventory (an inventory is more detailed), which supplies the date, description and reference number of each document or set of documents. There are indexes to some groups of records, but many records are not indexed. Also available are source lists which list records from various groups relating to particular subjects, eg Canada, Coal Mining, Military records.

4.5 Whenever a group of records or series of documents or individual document is mentioned in this book, its reference number will be given in brackets. You should keep a similar note of the reference numbers of the documents which provide you with information.

4.6 To see a document, you order it by means of an order slip on which you write its reference (or call) number, your name, the date, and the number of your seat in the search room. You must write a separate slip for each reference number. You may order a maximum of three at one time.

Order slip used in Historical and West Search Rooms

4.7 Most of the inventories and repertories will have an introductory note and contents list. If there is no contents list, see if the Summary Catalogue supplies this defect. Modern inventories and repertories are done to a common form, with the reference numbers in the left-hand margin (see *illustration*). In older catalogues, which vary in form, the reference number of each document may not be immediately apparent.

Reference	
CH2/1244	TONGLAND kirk session
1.	Minutes 1822–41 　　　　1857–65
2.	1866–1909
3.	Accounts 1748–56 Minute of meeting anent parochial school fees, 8 Sept. 1803
4.	Cash book 1822–52
5.	1858–85 Proclamations 1858–86
6.	Cash book 1903–12
7.	Baptismal register 1863–1930
8.	Proclamation register 1879–1956
9.	Communion roll 1860–8
10.	1875–80
11.	1881–96
12.	1896–1905
13.	1906–35
14.	1936–48
15.	List of men in active service 1917
16.	Miscellaneous papers 19–20 cent.

Page in an SRO repertory

4.8 Indexes vary tremendously in quality and style. Pre-20th century manuscript 'indexes' may not be indexes in our understanding of the word, sometimes being contents list, and sometimes alphabetical only as far as the first letter of each surname.

4.9 Surnames beginning with 'Mc' or 'Mac' may be indexed as if 'Mc' (or 'Mac') was a separate letter of the alphabet or may be combined with the letter 'M' in the English fashion. On very rare occasions, they may be indexed by the letter following the 'Mc', ie 'Macdonald' would be found under the letter 'D' (eg in LC.9/3/1).

4.10 'Mc' means 'son of' and in the Highlands and Islands until the 18th century its appearance in a name might mean just that. Duncan Dow McEan VcEwen was the son of Ean (John) and grandson of Ewen (Dow being a nickname meaning 'black'). Duncan's son would probably bear the name 'McDonachie' or a variant thereof. Similarly, in the Northern Isles, particularly Shetland, Andrew Davidson could be the son of David Manson, who was the son of Magnus. It is difficult to specify a date when such 'patronymics' stuck as modern surnames.

4.11 In Scotland, a woman does not 'change her name' on marriage. Thus, married women are usually described in documents and indexed under their maiden name or, more recently, with alternative surnames (eg Mary Stewart, wife of William Sim; Mary Stewart or Sim).

4.12 In the older catalogues and indexes, two types of numerals may be used: roman numbers (i, ii, iii, iv, etc) and our conventional arabic numbers (1, 2, 3, 4, etc). If these numbers are part of a reference or call number, convert a roman number into an arabic number, when ordering out or referring to a document.

4.13 Surnames and place-names in catalogues are usually spelled in the form in which they are found in the document. Some indexes modernise names, some do not. Look under all possible variants of the surname you are seeking.

4.14 Most catalogues and indexes give not only the Christian name(s) and surname of each individual but also his 'designation'. This designation may include his occupation, where he lives, or a relationship, usually the name and designation of his father: eg John Fulton, bonnet-maker in Kilmarnock; George Duncan, son of John D., portioner of Auchtermuchty ('portioner' means he owned part of these lands).

4.15 Some of the more important records are public registers, which may consist not only of volumes, but also of 'warrants'. A warrant is the authority for certain information to be put into the register. Sometimes the warrant is an original document which has been copied into a volume of the register.

4.16 You will soon become accustomed to variant and eccentric spellings in the documents you read. Newcomers to research in Scottish documents will encounter two other particular problems. The first is that documents before the 18th century were written in unfamiliar scripts, with many letter forms different from those we use today. Learning to read these older scripts is quite easy, but does take practice. Useful books are *Scottish Handwriting 1150-1650* by Grant G Simpson (Aberdeen University Press, 1977) and *Scottish Handwriting 1500-1700: a self-help pack* by Alison Rosie (Scottish Record Office and Scottish Records Association, 1994). If you live in or near Edinburgh, you might like to attend an evening class on Scottish Handwriting held in General Register House each winter under the auspices of the Extra-Mural Studies Department of Edinburgh University.

4.17 The second problem is the language in which documents are written. Until recently, many Scottish documents were written in Scots, a form of English with its own vocabulary and phraseology. This is where a dictionary becomes invaluable. More awkwardly, until well on in the 19th century, important legal documents were in Latin. However, a very small knowledge of Latin and some practice in recognising the salient parts of such documents can help considerably. In post-medieval Latin documents, surnames and place-names are mostly in Scots and English.

4.18 In subsequent chapters, advice is given on how to search relevant groups of records. There is one group of records which appears in most chapters and therefore it is convenient to describe it here. That group consists of records known as Gifts and Deposits (GD), which are the records of private individuals, families, organisations and business concerns, which have been gifted or are on loan to the SRO. They contain an infinite variety of record and information and often supplement other groups of records. Look at the index to the Summary Catalogue to see if they include a collection of papers in which you are interested and if there is a catalogue of that particular collection. A few of the GDs are also described in two published volumes *List of Gifts and Deposits in the Scottish Record Office* (purchasable from the SRO). Smaller GDs are referenced as GD.1. Larger GDs each have their own reference number, eg the Earl of Airlie's records are GD.16. More than one hundred of the five hundred catalogues of private collections can now be searched on the SRO's own computer cataloguing and retrieval system called Clio. This system automatically indexes every word in any catalogue and allows you to search on words or combinations of words, on names, on dates and on reference numbers. Other collections of family and business papers may be found in local record offices (see Appendix A).

4.19 Of the GD collections, the most useful for you are probably those of the big landowning families, as the names of those who lived in their estates may appear among their estate papers. If you know the area where your ancestor lived, you may want to find out who were the landowners in that area. The parish reports printed in the *Old* and *New Statistical Accounts of Scotland* usually provide this information for the end of the 18th century and around 1840 respectively.

4.20 There is also a series of private records referenced RH.15. The titles of these collections are indexed both in the Summary Catalogue and in a separate RH.15 index. RH is the reference number for a varied series of records of mixed and sometimes uncertain origin. They include transcripts and photocopies (RH.2) and microfilms (RH.4) of various records held elsewhere than the SRO.

4.21 Photocopies of most documents may be purchased. Because of pressure of business, there may be a considerable delay before you receive the photocopies. Photocopies cost less when ordered and collected personally in the Search Room.

4.22 A small number of the records are closed to public access. These are recent government records, which may be closed for between 30 and 100 years, a few GD collections which the owner has placed under restriction, and collections which have not yet been catalogued.

4.23 The National Register of Archives (Scotland), which is a branch of the SRO, surveys private records kept elsewhere in Scotland. An index and copies of these surveys may be consulted in the SRO . If you want to consult documents mentioned in a survey, contact the secretary of the NRA(S) for further advice. However, papers which are still in private hands are often not available for genealogical research.

West Register House

$\mathscr{B}$irths, Baptisms, Marriages and Deaths

5.1 If you fail to find a record of baptism, marriage or death in New Register House, then you should look among the non-conformist church and other records in the SRO. It helps considerably if you know the religious denomination of your ancestor, as well as the essential information of the approximate place of residence. *The Old Statistical Account* is a useful source of information as to which denominations were active in particular parishes at the end of the 18th century. The books listed in 16.1 record the locations of most of the Presbyterian congregations which have existed in Scotland.

5.2 *If your ancestor was Protestant,* go to the repertory labelled CH. The non-conformist records are labelled CH.3 and CH.10-16, of which the bulkiest are CH.3, the records of the former free churches which have become re-united with the Church of Scotland.

5.3 Look at the index of churches, presbyteries and synods in CH.3 for the name of the likely congregation or name of the town and the congregation therein. This index will provide you with the reference number of the congregation's records, eg Milnathort Antiburgher church is CH.3/542. The CH.3 records are arranged in numerical order, so look in the CH.3 repertory under the relevant number. Within the list of records of that congregation, you will be looking for records of baptisms or marriages or deaths, either as separate volumes or in the same volumes as kirk session minutes: eg Lethendy Associate Congregation Session minute book (CH.3/214/1) includes baptisms, 1803-1840. The repertory will say if there is such a record: normally, minutes do not include such information. Remember that many of these congregations did not exist until 1843, when the Free Church was formed by the Disruption from the established Church of Scotland.

5.4 When you are ordering out a volume of these Church records, make sure that your order slip has three numbers, eg CH.3/214/1, the second number being the number of the congregation and the third the volume number.

5.5 Some of these church records have been transferred to local archives (Glasgow City, Stirling Council, etc) but the SRO has retained microfilms of many of those records prior to 1860, which microfilms may be consulted. Order the microfilm out by the CH reference number, adding the word 'microfilm'.

5.6 The Church records include records of some congregations of the Society of Friends or Quakers (CH.10) and Methodist (CH.11), Episcopal (CH.12), United Free (CH.13), Congregational (CH.14), Unitarian (CH.15) and Free (CH.16) churches. To search each of these, look at the introductory pages in the relevant volume of the CH repertory to see if the congregation you want is listed. Any records of births/baptisms, marriages and deaths/burials will be noted in the list of that congregation's records. Only a few of the records of these churches are in the SRO, but the SRO also has microfilm copies of Episcopal Church registers, arranged by diocese. Look at the RH.4 repertory at RH.4/179-185 and appendices 51-57 which list the registers. There is also a microfilm of the baptismal register of the Catholic Apostolic Church, Edinburgh, 1833-1949 (RH.4/174). If the records of the congregation you want are not in the SRO, look in the index to the surveys produced by the National Register of Archives (Scotland). Failing that, you should contact the headquarters of that particular church. The addresses of some will be found in *The Church of Scotland Year-Book*.

5.7 *If your ancestor was Roman Catholic,* go to the repertory labelled RH.21. Listed there are photocopies of the surviving records kept by Roman Catholic parish priests of baptisms, marriages and deaths. These are arranged by diocese, but there is an alphabetical list of the parishes at the start of the repertory, giving the reference number of each. The earliest date is 1703, but most registers do not start until the 19th century.

5.8 One has to emphasise the incompleteness of all these church records, their existence having depended on the dedication of the clergymen and accident of survival. They are also inconsistent in the details supplied.

5.9 Records of baptisms will usually give the names of the child and of the father, sometimes that of the mother, and in the case of the Roman Catholic records, sometimes those of the god-parents, who may be relatives. If the clergyman chooses, there may occasionally be additional information, eg '4th Sept Margaret Riccalton Dickson daughter of Walter Dickson (above 70 years of age) and his wife Eve Riccalton' (1833 – CH.3/667/1).

5.10 Records of marriages will generally give only the name of the marrying couple, but some RC registers invaluably give the parishes in Ireland from where the couple came.

5.11 There are very few death records among the CH.3 records and these usually only give the name of the deceased, sometimes the age. Because the Roman Catholic priest needed to give the last sacrament to a dying person, the RC records of deaths are fuller, usually giving the name, age, marital status and cause of death, eg 'John Carley, a married man, was suddenly suffocated in an old Coal pit at Campsie by Damp Air' (1815 June 27th – RH.21/62/10, p.251).

5.12 There are further records which provide evidence of the birth, marriage and decease of individuals.

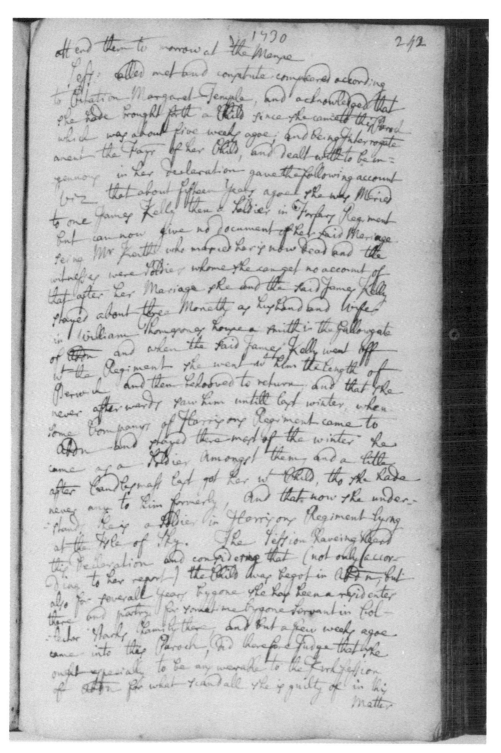

Married or unmarried? A mother's story, 1730. (CH.2/201/2)

Fornication

5.13   The records of both the Church of Scotland and the free churches report the appearance before the kirk session of couples whose extra-marital fornication had resulted in the birth of a child. How to gain access to the records of the free churches is already described (5.3). Access to the records of the kirk sessions of the Church of Scotland (CH.2) is similar. Go to the volume of the CH.2 repertory which contains an index of the parishes etc listed in the repertory. Each parish has a reference number. Look up the volumes listed under that number: each volume has its own number. Order the relevant volume of the kirk session minutes by its reference number, eg CH.2/842/2. Such misbehaviour by unmarried couples (whether or not a child was the result) seems to have been the main concern of many kirk sessions prior to 1900 and their minute books may contain little else. The name of the child will not be given but you will find proof of the birth of a child to a named mother and, with luck, father and the approximate date of birth. An occasional problem arises when the name of the father given by the mother appears to be false. Such entries sometimes demonstrate that the unmarried mother had recently arrived from another parish (*see illustration*).

Aliment

5.14   Further evidence of illegitimate births may be found in actions before a sheriff court to order the father to contribute to the maintenance of the child. The record of these actions for aliment will usually provide the names of the mother and father and the date of birth and sex, but not the name, of the child. See 11.36-41 for further explanation of these sheriff court records, which are largely unindexed.

Adoption

5.15   Adoption was not recognised in the law of Scotland until 1930. There are records of adoption in the Court of Session records (CS.312) and Sheriff Court records, but information may only be supplied from these records to the adopted child having reached the age of 17 or by order of the Court of Session or Sheriff Court concerned.

Legitimation

5.16   The disciplinary procedures of the kirk sessions show that many children were born illegitimate. Some were legitimated by the subsequent marriage of the parents. Others might be legitimated by the Crown or as a consequence of a court declaration.

5.17   Legitimations by the Crown are contained, along with other business, in the records of the Privy Seal (PS). A calendar of these records has been published for the years 1488-1584 in 8 volumes, *The Register of the Privy Seal of Scotland*. Each of these volumes has an index of persons, which will lead you to an entry in the calendar. At the end of the entry, there is a roman numeral and an arabic numeral, representing respectively the volume and folio number of the original entry in the Privy Seal record. To see the original, which will be in Latin, you order by the reference number PS. 1 and the volume number, coverting it into an arabic numeral (eg PS.1/11). For the period between 1585 and 1660, there is no index and you have to use the Privy Seal minute books (PS.6/3 and 4), which are written in order of entry in the Register and give only the surname of the person concerned (and what he has been granted, such as legitimation) but provide the volume and folio number in the register (PS.1). For the period since 1660, look at the 2-volume index to the Privy Seal 'English record' (ie written in English). The first volume, up to 1782, indexes persons without distinguishing legitimations, but the second volume does specify them. If you wish to see the original entry in the Privy Seal register, order by PS.3 and the volume number. Remember that legitimations might be granted at any age.

Constitution and Dissolution of Marriage

5.18 Legitimation can be proved in court by proving the marriage of the parents. Irregular marriages could be recognised by a court of law. Divorce has been possible in Scotland since 1560. From the Reformation until 1830, the court which was responsible for cases involving legitimation and the constitution and dissolution of marriage was the Commissary Court of Edinburgh (CC.8). Since 1830, the responsible court has been the Court of Session, though between 1831 and 1835 some cases were still dealt with by the Commissary Court.

5.19 A catalogue of such cases heard by the Commissary Court was published by the Scottish Record Society in 1909 – *The Commissariot of Edinburgh - Consistorial Processes and Decreets, 1658-1800*: which has an index of persons. The cases include adherence, declarator of marriage and legitimacy, separation and aliment, divorce, declarator of nullity of marriage, declarator of illegitimacy. In this catalogue, where the description of the case is followed by a roman, then an arabic, numeral, the roman numeral is that of a volume of decrees, which may be ordered by CC.8/5 plus the roman numeral (converted into arabic). The arabic numeral is that of the folio on which the report of the case starts. Unless the description includes the words 'no warrants', then the papers in the case will be among the consistorial processes and may be ordered by the reference number CC.8/6 and the number of whatever box contains the processes for the relevant date: these numbers may be obtained from the repertory of Commissary Court records (CC).

5.20 If you are looking for a case between 1800 and 1835, then order out an index referenced CC.8/6/176. This index is arranged alphabetically only by the initial of the pursuer's surname and chronologically within each letter of the alphabet. It describes the parties simply by their surnames, but a list of all the cases in a volume referenced CC.8/20/6 generally provides their Christian names and designations. Again, where there is a decree (CC.8/5), the index gives the volume and folio number, and where there is none, you must seek the process (CC.8/6) in the box for the relevant year, which the index gives.

5.21   For lawsuits regarding marriage, divorce and legitimacy heard by the Court of Session since 1830, you must go to the records of that Court (see 11.3-20).

Proclamation of Banns of Marriage

5.22   Before a regular marriage took place, the intention to marry had to be publicised by a proclamation in church. As the parties had to pay a fee, kirk session account and cash books sometimes give the names of couples about to marry, in such terms as 'To cash received from James Kirk in Auchterderran when contracted with Catherine Haxton in this Parish' (Kinglassie, 1783 June 6, CH.2/406/7). Unfortunately, many of these account book entries simply state 'Proclamation' and the amount paid, omitting the names of the parties. If you wish to follow this line of inquiry, the relevant records are listed in the CH.2 repertory, described in 5.13.

Marriage Contracts

5.23   Until recently, it was the practice, when members of propertied families got married, for a marriage contract to be drawn up, whereby the families made financial provision for the couple, particularly for the future financial security of the wife and children. These contracts could be drawn up either before or after the marriage ceremony. You would expect to find in a marriage contract the names of the couple and their fathers and possibly other relatives. The date of the contract would usually but not necessarily be close to the date of the marriage. As these were private documents, there is no guarantee that the one you are seeking has survived, but the following groups of records should be consulted.

5.24   Registers of Deeds (RD, SC, etc) - see 10.2-16. One difficulty in searching for marriage contracts in this source is that a marriage contract might be registered years after the date of the marriage, perhaps after the death of the husband. There was no compulsion to register a marriage contract.

5.25   Register of Sasines (RS). As many marriage contracts included provisions for a liferent income from land, the subsequent instrument of sasine should be recorded in a Register of Sasines - see 8.3-18.

5.26   Gifts and Deposits (GD). If either of the parties was a member of a family whose records have been gifted to or deposited in the SRO, then their marriage contract may be among these records - see 4.18. The card index to the miscellaneous accessions referenced GD.1 includes references to marriage contracts in that collection of records.

5.27 Miscellaneous papers – Marriage Contracts (RH.9/7). This is a collection of 306 marriage contracts with no other common denominator. They are arranged and listed in two series, the first chronological from 1591 to 1846 and the second rather haphazardly arranged but dated between 1605 and 1811. They are not indexed but are clearly catalogued in the RH.9 repertory.

5.28 One should bear in mind that occasionally a marriage contract was not followed by a marriage (see 11.55).

Irregular Marriages

5.29 Until 1940, irregular marriages, in the form of a declaration by the parties before witnesses, but not before an established clergyman, were perfectly legal. However, such marriages were frowned upon. The parties might be rebuked by their kirk session and they and their witnesses were liable to be fined. Thus evidence of such marriages may be found in kirk session minutes described in 5.13 and in burgh and JP court records (see 11.46-48). They are further explained in the introduction to *Calendar of Irregular Marriages in the South Leith Kirk Session Records 1697-1818* (Scottish Record Society). The Ewart Library in Dumfries is the best source of information about irregular marriages at Gretna Green. The SRO has copies of registers of similar marriages at Lamberton Toll, Berwickshire, 1833-1849 (RH.2/8/84).

Inhibitions

5.30 Evidence of marriage might also appear when a husband stopped his liability for his wife's debts (see 11.56-58).

Fatal Accidents

5.31 The Fatal Accidents Inquiry (Scotland) Act, 1895, provided for public inquiries by sheriff and jury into fatal accidents occurring in industrial employment or occupations. If you are looking for information about a fatal accident at work, you should look at the repertory of the records of the relevant sheriff court (see 11.36). The contents list will give you the reference number of the fatal accident inquiry records. There are none earlier than 1895. You should find the name of the widow, employment and employers of the deceased, and the date and cause of death. These records are not indexed.

Mortcloth and Burial Records

5.32 It used to be common for the kirk session of the parish church to hire out a mortcloth to cover a dead body during the funeral service. The kirk session accounts, by recording a payment for a mortcloth, give the approximate date of death of the corpse. Records of mortcloth payments may appear in the kirk session minutes or account books (CH2 - see 5.13) or in the accounts kept by the heritors (HR - see 8.41). Such accounts may also include payments for coffins or digging the grave of named persons.

Account of mortcloth money, 1765. (CH.2/181/9)

5.33 A few of the CH.2 kirk session records include records of burials, specified in
the list of records of that kirk session. Among the burgh records in the SRO,
there are cemetery records for Dunbar, 1879-1902 (B.18/18/24) and Tranent,
1885-1949 (B.77/5/2-4). However, cemetery reccords are mostly held by the
District Council in whose area the cemetery lies and enquiries in the first
instance should be made to the Chief Executive or Superintendent of
Cemeteries of the appropriate district council. The SRO holds very few
district council records and the only burial records therein are those of
Prestonpans - look up DC.2/5/23-28 in the District Council repertory (DC).
Such burial records may be more concerned with the purchaser of a place of
burial than with who is actually buried there.

5.34 The records of the Edinburgh Cemetery Company, which administered seven cemeteries in the city and which were formerly held on temporary deposit by the SRO, have now been transferred permanently to Edinburgh City Archives.

5.35 The inscriptions on gravestones are usually of great genealogical value. The microfilm series (RH.4) includes copies of monumental inscriptions noted by S Cramer in burial grounds in various parts of Scotland (RH.4/16 and 41). Look at Appendix 13 in the RH.4 repertory for the full list of these burial grounds.

5.36 A consistent survey of monumental inscriptions throughout Scotland is being compiled on behalf of the Scottish Genealogy Society. These are bound in volumes by county or part-county, in which the arrangement is by alphabetical order of churchyard with an index of surnames for each churchyard. A similar series of monumental inscriptions in Cunninghame District has been compiled by the district council. Copies of all these volumes are in the SRO library - look up the library card index, topographical drawers, under the name of the relevant county to obtain the reference number.

Anatomy

5.37 Not all bodies go directly to their grave. Some are supplied to schools of anatomy for the benefit of the students . Since 1842, the Inspector of Anatomy for Scotland has kept registers which are preserved in the SRO as part of the records of the Ministry of Health. Look at the MH repertory where these registers are listed under the reference MH.1. There were schools of anatomy at Aberdeen, Dundee, Edinburgh, Glasgow and St Andrews. There is a 50 year closure period on this record. The registers are arranged chronologically and give the name, age, sex, last place of abode (typically the Royal Infirmary or Charity Workhouse), and date, place and cause of death, of each deceased. The registers are not indexed.

6

Inheritance: Wills and Executries

6.1 Apart from the records of births, marriages and deaths, the most useful records for genealogical research are those which deal with inheritance and the disposal of the property of a deceased person. In legal terms, property may be either heritable or moveable, and, until 1964, the rules of inheritance in Scotland were different in respect of heritable and moveable property. Heritable property is basically land, minerals in the ground, and buildings. Moveable property is basically property that can be moved, such as money, furniture, animals, machinery and implements. Because of this distinction, the information about inheritance in heritable and moveable property is kept in different records and therefore is best considered separately. In this chapter, we shall consider the records which concern the disposal of moveable property of a person who has died.

6.2 When a person dies, an executor should be appointed to administer the moveable estate of the deceased. If the deceased has left a will, then the executor will usually be appointed by the will, though this appointment will require confirmation by the relevant court. If the deceased has died intestate, then the executor will be appointed and confirmed by the court. Thus the records which concern us are the records of the confirmation of executors, whether or not there is a will. These records are known as testaments, a testament-testamentar if there is a will, a testament–dative if there is none. Each testament will give the name and designation of the deceased, usually the date of death, the confirmation of the executor, an inventory of the moveable estate of the deceased (which may include household furniture, implements of trade, and debts owed to and by the deceased), and the will, if there is one.

6.3 The relevant court was a commissary court (CC) until the 1820s and there after a sheriff court (SC). Obviously, before you search for the will or executry of an ancestor, you must first know the approximate year of death and where in Scotland he or she lived.

6.4 Before investigating the relevant records,'you should be aware of certain snags.

    a.   Not only did very few people leave wills, but, in the majority of cases, the family of a deceased person did not bother with the formality of confirming an executry. 'We keepit siller in the crap o' the wa', jist stappit in. We had nae lawyers, a'body just fechted it oot amang themselves.' (*Innes Review*, vol. VII, no. 11).

b.   Some records have not survived because of the depredations of fire and other accidents.

c.   As an eldest son inherited the whole of the heritable property of his deceased father, he did not receive any of the moveable property in intestacy and therefore the eldest son's name may be omitted from his father's testament.

d.   If the deceased had died in debt, his nearest of kin might not wish to take on his executry (and therefore liability to his creditors). Thus sometimes a creditor is named as executor. In such a case, the testament is unlikely to contain genealogical information.

e.   Testaments are usually confirmed within a year of death, but this is not always so, eg Captain James Carmichael died at Nairn on 17 May 1813 but his executry was not confirmed until 30 October 1827 (SC.26/39/1, p. 326).

Executries before 1801

6.5 If your ancestor died before 1801, then the relevant court is a commissary court. There are records for 22 such courts covering different parts of Scotland. The commissary courts acquired the jurisdiction of the pre-Reformation church courts and the areas they administered (known as commissariots) were based on the areas of these church courts, which are different from any modern administrative areas.

6.6 Therefore, you should first find out which commissary court or courts cover the area in which your ancestor lived. A useful series of maps published by the Institute of Heraldic and Genealogical Studies, Northgate, Canterbury, Kent, gives the boundaries of the commissariots and the parishes which were then within them: a set of these maps is kept in the Historical Search Room. Other guides to which parishes were in which commissariots are mentioned in 2.4. However, changes in parish boundaries and the irregularity of the bounds of the commissariots mean that it may be easier for you to use the following table which simply shows modern counties and their equivalent commissariots. (There is a similar table at the start of the CC repertory.) It is always advisable to check the commissary court of Edinburgh as well as the local commissary court, as, while Edinburgh dealt mainly with the executries of people who lived within the commissariot of Edinburgh, it could also confirm the executors of people who lived elsewhere and particularly those who died furth of Scotland.

County	Commissariot	Reference Number
Aberdeen	Aberdeen	CC.1
	Moray	CC.16
Augus (Forfar)	Brechin	CC.3
	Dunkeld	CC.7
	St Andrews	CC.20

County	Commissariot	Reference Number
Argyll	Argyll	CC.2
	The Isles	CC.12
Ayr	Glasgow	CC.9
Banff	Aberdeen	CC.1
	Moray	CC.16
Berwick	Lauder	CC.15
Bute	The Isles	CC.12
Caithness	Caithness	CC.4
Clackmannan	Dunblane	CC.6
	Stirling	CC.21
Dumfries	Dumfries	CC.5
Dunbarton	Glasgow	CC.9
	Hamilton and Campsie	CC.10
East Lothian (Haddington)	Edinburgh	CC.8
	Dunkeld	CC.7
Edinburgh city	Edinburgh	CC.8
Fife	Dunkeld	CC.7
	St Andrews	CC.20
	Stirling	CC.21
Glasgow city	Glasgow	CC.9
	Hamilton and Campsie	CC.10
Inverness	Argyll	CC.2
	Inverness	CC.11
	The Isles	CC.12
	Moray	CC.16
Kincardine	Brechin	CC.3
	St Andrews	CC.20
Kinross	St Andrews	CC.20
	Stirling	CC.21
Kirkcudbright	Dumfries	CC.5
	Kirkcudbright	CC.13
	Wigtown	CC.22
Lanark	Glasgow	CC.9
	Hamilton and Campsie	CC.10
	Lanark	CC.14
Midlothian (Edinburgh)	Edinburgh	CC.8
Moray (Elgin)	Moray	CC.16
Nairn	Moray	CC.16
Orkney	Orkney and Shetland	CC.17
Peebles	Peebles	CC.18
Perth	Dunblane	CC.6
	Dunkeld	CC.7
	St Andrews	CC.20
Renfrew	Glasgow	CC.9
	Hamilton and Campsie	CC.10
Ross and Cromarty	The Isles	CC.12
	Ross	CC.19

County	Commissariot	Reference Number
Roxburgh	Peebles	CC.18
Selkirk	Peebles	CC.18
Shetland	Orkney and Shetland	CC.17
Stirling	Glasgow	CC.9
	Hamilton and Campsie	CC.10
	Stirling	CC.21
Sutherland	Caithness	CC.4
West Lothian (Linlithgow)	Edinburgh	CC.8
	Dunkeld	CC.7
Wigtown	Wigtown	CC.22

6.7 There is a printed index for each commissariot containing the names of all the persons whose executry was confirmed up to 1800 and for whom the record has survived. Each index gives the name and designation of the deceased and the date of confirmation, which you should note carefully. Always check the end of the index in case additional information has been added. Married women are indexed under their maiden name with a cross-reference from the name of their husband. These indexes to the 'Commissariot Records', published by the Scottish Record Society in 1897-1904, are now out of-print but should be available through a library, as well as being available for consultation in the SRO.

6.8 Having found the name of your ancestor in one of these indexes, you now want to convert the name of the commissariot and the date of the confirmation into a reference number. To do so you must consult the CC repertory. Each commissary court has its own reference number (eg CC.7) as listed in the table above and also in the introduction to the repertory. Look in the repertory for the pages which list the records under that reference number. These pages will start with a contents list, which will give you the reference number of the Register of Testaments (eg CC.7/6). Turn to the page with that reference number and you will find the volumes of the Register listed with covering dates. Select the volume of which the dates include the date of confirmation you have noted in the index. For example, in the index to the Commissariot of Glasgow testaments, there is an entry for 'Wilson, George, merchant, burgess of Glasgow' with the date '25 Oct. 1614'. The reference number for the Glasgow Register of Testaments is CC.9/7. Volume 10 is dated 1614 June 2-1615 Aug. 17. Therefore, you order CC.9/7/10.

6.9 The index has given you a date, not a folio or page number. Having obtained the relevant volume, check first to see if there is a contents list at the beginning or end of the volume. If there is no contents list and the chances are that there will not be, you have to select a likely part of the volume and browse through it to find the testament you want. As most volumes are arranged chronologically by dates of confirmation, it should not be too difficult to choose the correct part of the volume. The name of the deceased is usually placed clearly in the margin, sometimes with the date of confirmation, or the date of confirmation should appear in the last or second last paragraph of the testament. There is often no gap between one testament and the next, so look for the words 'The Testament'

('Dative' or 'Testamentar') which starts each testament. The testament of George Wilson, mentioned above, provides the names of his wife and five children, three of whom must have been under 14 years of age, because the will appoints tutors to them ('Tutors' are explained in 7.5.).

6.10 Sometimes, a volume of a register of testaments has not survived but related documents called 'warrants' (see 4.15) have done so. The index should make this clear, usually by placing a letter 'T' before the data relating to a warrant. In such an instance, instead of looking in the CC repertory for the reference number of a register of testaments, you must look for the reference number of the warrants of testaments. This reference number will be to a box or bundle of warrants which will include the one you want. Where a series of testaments or warrants is lacking, other papers in the commissary records, for example edicts, may provide details such as the names of executors.

6.11 The Register of Testaments and most other records of Aberdeen Commissary Court were destroyed by fire in 1722. Afterwards, copies of some earlier testaments and other writs were collected into a series now referenced CC.1/15. These are not indexed but are listed in a minute book (CC.1/11/9). The testaments date back into the 17th century.

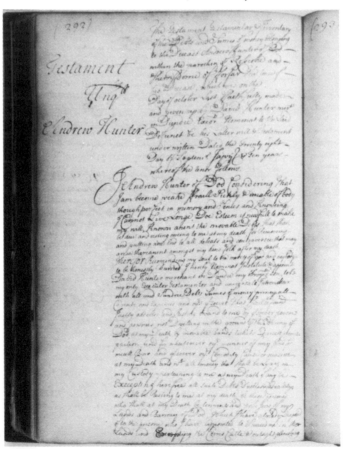

Page from Register of Testaments, 1710. (CC. 20/4/17)

Executries between 1801 and the 1820s

6.12 By the Commissary Courts (Scotland) Act, 1823, the commissary courts ceased to exist on 1 January 1824 and their jurisdiction in executry matters was transferred to the sheriff courts, except that Edinburgh, Haddington and Linlithgow remained part of the commissariot of Edinburgh until 1830. However, as far as the records are concerned, the transfer was not made precisely and there is considerable overlap between the testamentary records of the commissary courts and those of the sheriff courts, both before and after January 1824. This overlap is made clear in the following table of indexes, which explains in which commissary or sheriff court index you should search for an executry, if your ancestor lived in a particular county of Scotland between 1801 and 1829. Owing to the idiosyncrasy of the areas administered by the commissary courts and the overlap between the testamentary records kept by the commissary and sheriff courts, it may be necessary to check several indexes and records to find the record of a particular executry. Further information about the commissary indexes is in 6.13 and about the sheriff court indexes in 6.14-23.

County	Commissariot index	Sheriff Court index
Aberdeen	General index (to 1827)	sc.1 (from 1824)
Angus (Forfar)	St Andrews index (to 1823)	sc.47 (from 1824)
	General index (to 1823)	
Argyll	General index (to 1823)	sc.51 (from 1815)
Ayr	Glasgow index (to 1823)	sc.6 (from 1824)
Banff	General index (to 1827)	sc.2 (from 1824)
Berwick	General index (to 1827)	sc.60 (from 1823)
Bute	General index (to 1823)	sc.8 (from 1824)
Caithness	General index (to 1827)	sc.14 (from 1829)
		(but record from 1824)
Clackmannan	General index (to 1825)	sc.64 (from 1824)
Dumfries	General index (to 1829)	sc.15 (from 1827)
Dunbarton	Glasgow index (to 1823)	sc.65 (from 1824)
	General index (to 1823)	
East Lothian	Edinburgh index (to 1829)	sc.70 (1808-1829
(Haddington)	Index 1804-1808 to cc.8/11	- 2 indexes)
	General index (to 1823)	
Edinburgh city	Edinburgh index (to 1829)	sc.70 (from 1808
	Index 1804-1808 to cc.8/11	- 2 indexes)
Fife	St Andrews index (to 1823)	sc.20 (from 1824)
	General index (to 1823)	
Glasgow city	Glasgow index (to 1823)	sc.36 (from 1824)
	General index (to 1823)	
Inverness	General index (to 1827)	sc.29 (from 1825)
	Index 1820-1824 to cc.11/1/9	
Kincardine	St Andrews index (to 1823)	sc.5 (from 1824)
	General index (to 1823)	

County	Commissariot index	Sheriff Court index
Kinross	St Andrews index (to 1823) General index (to 1825)	SC.64 (from 1824)
Kirkcudbright	General index (to 1829)	SC.16 (from 1824)
Lanark	Glasgow index (to 1823) General index (to 1823)	SC.36 (from 1824)
Midlothian (Edinburgh)	Edinburgh index (to 1829) Index 1804-1808 to CC.8/11	SC.70 (from 1808-2 indexes)
Moray (Elgin)	General index (to 1827)	SC.26 (from 1824)
Nairn	General index (to 1827)	SC.26 (from 1824)
Orkney	Orkney indexes (2 indexes, 1806-1823 and 1809-1831)	[SC records from 1824 are kept in Kirkwall]
Peebles	Peebles index (to 1827)	SC.42 (from 1814)
Perth	St Andrews index (to 1823) General index (to 1825)	SC.44 (from 1824) SC.49 (from 1824)
Renfrew	Glasgow index (to 1823) General index (to 1823)	SC.58 (from 1824)
Ross and Cromarty	General index (to 1824)	SC.25 (from 1824) SC.33 (from 1827)
Roxburgh	Peebles index (to 1827)	SC.62 (from 1827)
Selkirk	Peebles index (to 1827)	SC.63 (from 1824)
Shetland	Index 1811-1826 to CC.17/5/6	[SC.records from 1827 are kept in Lerwick
Stirling	Glasgow index (to 1823) General index (to 1823)	SC.67 (from 1809)
Sutherland	General index (to 1827)	[No index. Record is SC.9/36, from 1799]
West Lothian (Linlithgow)	Edinburgh index (to 1829) Index 1804-1808 to CC.8/11 General index (to 1823)	SC.70 (1808-1829-2 indexes)
Wigtown	General index (to 1823) Index 1810-1826 to CC.22/4	[No index. Record is SC.19/41, from 1826]

6.13 For executries between 1801 and 1823, the appropriate court should be the commissary court. If you know in which county your ancestor lived, use the table above to find out which indexes to consult. If you fail to find any information in these indexes, remember that it is also worth checking the indexes to the Edinburgh commissary records. As you will see from the table above, there are different indexes to the post-1800 commissary records from those which were described in 6.7. There are several post-1800 indexes, mostly in typescript. There are separate indexes for each of the commissariots of Edinburgh, Glasgow, Orkney, Peebles and St Andrews. There is a combined index for all the other commissariots: its introductory pages include a list of abbreviations. These indexes give the name and designation of the deceased, the date of confirmation, the commissariot, and the volume and folio numbers or warrant number of the testament. Unless the information has been added to the index, you must look at the CC repertory to discover the reference number of that volume or warrant, eg 'ADDISON, James, baker, Dundee, 1814 March 8, Brechin vol. 14 fol. 40' will be found when you order out CC.3/3/14; and 'ADIE, Alexander, in Clachriach, 1802 April 2, Aberdeen W.63' will be found when you order out CC.1/6/65/63 (which is a warrant). As the index tells you the folio number on which the testament starts, once you have the volume, you can go straight to the relevant folio (unlike the pre-1800 testaments).

Executries between 1820s and 1875

6.14 The sheriff courts were now responsible for the confirmation of executors. Each sheriff court had its own way of organising its executry (or commissary) records, so that these records are not arranged consistently. Sometimes there are three separate series of commissary records, all of which you may wish to examine, but sometimes two or all three series may be combined. Though the names they were given also vary (eg 'commissary record books'), the basic three are records of confirmations (of executries), wills ('settlements', 'testamentary deeds'), and inventories (of the moveable estate of the deceased). Thus, you must look very carefully at each repertory of sheriff court records to ascertain which record or records you need to consult. Remember that if your ancestor died intestate, then there will be no will.

6.15 When a person lived outwith Scotland, but died leaving moveable property within Scotland, then confirmation of the executry was the responsibility of the commissary office of the sheriff court of Edinburgh (SC.70). If your ancestor resided within Scotland, then to find details of his executry, you must first know which sheriff court was responsible for the area in which he lived. *Index to Sheriff Court Districts in Scotland* by Charles McCaffray (W Green & Son, Edinburgh) contains an alphabetical index of cities, towns and villages in Scotland, showing the relevant sheriff court of each in 1980. Changes in sheriff courts in the last century limit its usefulness, but it may help you. The following table shows each modern county and the equivalent sheriff court which dealt with commissary business between the 1820s and 1875.

County	Sheriff Court	Reference number
Aberdeen	Aberdeen	SC.1
Angus (Forfar)	Dundee (from 1832)	SC.45
	Forfar	SC.47
Argyll	Dunoon	SC.51
Ayr	Ayr	SC.6
Banff	Banff	SC.2
Berwick	Duns	SC.60
Bute	Rothesay	SC.8
Caithness	Wick	SC.14
Clackmannan	Alloa	SC.64
Dumfries	Dumfries	SC.15
Dunbarton	Dumbarton	SC.65

County	Sheriff Court	Reference number
East Lothian (Haddington)	Haddington (from 1830)	SC.40
Edinburgh city	Edinburgh	SC.70
Fife	Cupar	SC.20
Glasgow city	Glasgow	SC.36
Inverness	Inverness	SC.29
Kincardine	Stonehaven	SC.5
Kinross	Alloa (to 1847)	SC.64
	Kinross (from 1847)	SC.22
Kirkcudbright	Kirkcudbright	SC.16
Lanark	Glasgow	SC.36
Midlothian (Edinburgh)	Edinburgh	SC.70
Moray (Elgin)	Elgin	SC.26
Nairn	Elgin (to 1838)	SC.26
	Nairn (from 1839)	SC.31
Orkney	Kirkwall	[In Kirkwall]
Peebles	Peebles	SC.42
Perth	Dunblane	SC.44
	Perth	SC.49
Renfrew	Paisley	SC.58
Ross	Dingwall	SC.25
	Stornoway (to 1850)	SC.33
Roxburgh	Jedburgh	SC.62
Selkirk	Selkirk	SC.63
Shetland	Lerwick	[In Lerwick]
Stirling	Stirling	SC.67
Sutherland	Dornoch	SC.9
West Lothian (Linlithgow)	Linlithgow (from 1830)	SC.41
Wigtown	Wigtown	SC.19

6.16 Having decided which is the relevant sheriff court, you must now look at the relevant index. There are three categories of index, described in 6.17, 6.18–19 and 6.20 respectively.

6.17 If the sheriff court is Cupar, Dingwall, Dunblane, Dunoon, Haddington, Linlithgow, Paisley, Perth, Stirling or Stornoway, then for each of these you will find a modern typed index adjacent to the repertory of the records of that sheriff court. All of these indexes relate to records which combine both inventories and wills in one volume, all give the volume and folio numbers for each executry, none has the modern reference number in the text of the index, but it is always written on an introductory page. Note, however, that the indexes to Cupar, Linlithgow and Perth give out-of-date volume numbers. For these sheriff courts, you must note the date of registration in the index, look up the relevant SC repertory and choose the volume which includes that date.

6.18 If your ancestor lived within the jurisdiction of any other sheriff court in Scotland and died between 1846 and 1867, or in the case of Edinburgh,

Haddington and Linlithgow, between 1827 and 1865, you should look at a series of printed indexes entitled *Index to Personal Estates of Defuncts*. (As these cover the whole of Scotland, they can also be used to cross-check the indexes mentioned in 6.17.) Look at the spines of these index volumes to find which includes the county you want. In these indexes, the deceased are indexed in alphabetical order, except that, within each surname, the men are listed before the women. Each name is followed by a designation, and, if the person died away from home, then that information is added, eg 'H 154 Cleland, John, captain of the "Mayflower", Port-Glasgow – died at Santa Cruz, 58.R.28.3.56'. As you see, the entry contains various letters and numbers. The first letter, before the name, tells you whether the deceased died testate or intestate (see the introduction to the index). Ignore the number which follows that letter. The number which immediately follows the designation is the year in which the inventory was recorded, ie '58' is 1858. The letter which follows tells you the relevant county, which in the case of John Cleland is 'R' for Renfrew (which means that his executry was administered by the sheriff court at Paisley). The final numbers are the date of death, so that John Cleland died on 28 March 1856.

6.19 The *Indexes to Personal Estates of Defuncts* index the inventories of the estates of the deceased. To proceed from the index, you find the relevant sheriff court repertory and look in the contents list for the 'Commissary Court' records, find therein the reference number of the record of inventories and look up that part of the repertory, where you will find the volumes listed with covering dates. You know the year of inventory and the date of death, so order out the volume or volumes which cover that year subsequent to the date of death. Thus, to find the inventory of the said John Cleland, you will order out the volume referenced SC.58/42/24. From the index at the start of that volume, you will find that Cleland's inventory starts on page 513. John Cleland was intestate, but if the deceased was testate and that particular sheriff court kept the wills in a separate series from the inventories, you will then have to ascertain which volume of wills to order out (see 6.22).

6.20 If your ancestor lived in a sheriffdom other than those specified in 6.17, and his executry was confirmed before 1846 or between 1868 and 1875, then you have to look at manuscript indexes which were compiled in the sheriffdoms. The original indexes for Edinburgh, Forfar and Jedburgh, and xerox copies for the other sheriff courts are kept beside their respective SC repertories. There are certain points to bear in mind in using these indexes.

i.   The xerox copies are of indexes in individual volumes of the record and to individual volumes. Therefore ensure that you are looking at the right index for the date you want. The covering dates of the volume will usually be added at the top of each index page.
ii.   For several sheriff courts outwith the central belt, the xeroxed 'indexes' are not actually indexes, but are contents lists .
iii.   The rest are only indexes to the extent that they arrange all surnames under their initial letter. Within each initial letter, the order is chronological.

iv.   The Edinburgh, Forfar and Jedburgh indexes give the relevant volume and folio number. The xeroxed indexes give only the folio number, but at the top of each page is added the covering dates of the volume, specifying what series it is in. You then have to go to the repertory to work out which volume you need to order.

v.   The index may not tell you if the person died testate or intestate.

6.21   Let us assume that your ancestor was Andrew Dearey, shipmaster in Aberdeen. You find his name in the SC.1 xeroxed index on a page headed 'Register of Inventories 1835'. You look up the SC.1 repertory, find that the Register of Inventories is referenced SC.1/36 and that the 1835 inventories are in volume 12, so that you order SC.1/36/12. The index tells you that his inventory starts on page 726. Therein you will read *inter alia* that Dearey died in Wapping on 7 November 1834, the names of his executors and that he left a will. To see the will you go back to the SC.1 repertory to find that the Register of Wills is SC.1/37 and the volume therein for 1835 is SC.1/37/12. This volume has an index, so that you can find that Dearey's will commences on page 539. If the volume had lacked an index or contents list, you would assume that the date of recording of the will would be close to the date of the inventory and look in that part of the volume, which is arranged chronologically. In Dearey's inventory, it also says that his will was registered in the Sheriff Court Books of Aberdeenshire on 26 December 1834. These sheriff court books are the Register of Deeds of the Aberdeen Sheriff Court (see further in 6.30) and you will find another copy of the will in the volume of that Register of Deeds referenced SC.1/62/36.

6.22   Let us take another example. You find from the *Index to Personal Estates of Defuncts* that the executry of Andrew Forsyth, builder in Elgin, was confirmed in 1848 in the sheriff court of Elgin. You look up the SC.26 repertory, find that its register of inventories is SC.26/39 and that the volume which includes 1848 is SC.26/39/6. The 'index' (contents list) in that volume tells you that Forsyth's inventory starts on page 61. You know from the index (and the inventory reminds you) that Forsyth was testate and so you look for his will in the volume of the SC.26 register of wills which covers the date of the inventory, 10 May 1848. This is SC.26/38/6, which includes a contents list which tells you that the will starts on page 282.

6.23   If your ancestor lived furth of Scotland, but owned property in Scotland, then the sheriff court of Edinburgh (SC.70) was responsible for his executry. If his executry was confirmed before 1858 or you simply want to see the inventory of his Scottish property, then you search as if he had died in Edinburgh. If the executry was confirmed between 1858 and 1900 and he lived in England or Ireland, then look at the typed index to the Probates Resealed, which are simply copies of the English and Irish probates. They have a running number which the index does not give, but it does give a date. You must look up the SC.70 repertory under SC.70/6 and find the reference number which includes that date. These probates do not include the inventory of goods belonging to the deceased in Scotland. That information is in the Edinburgh Register of Inventories (SC.70/1).

Executries since 1876

6.24 If your ancestor died after 1875, then your searching task is easier. From 1876 to 1959, there is a series of annual printed volumes called *Calendar of Confirmations and Inventories*. The Historical Search Room has a set of them up to 1929: thereafter the series may be consulted in the Legal Search Room (but any sheriff court records should still be ordered out in the Historical Search Room). This *Calendar* indexes all those persons whose executry has been confirmed in Scotland in that particular year, regardless of where they lived. The index is in strict alphabetical order, except that some entries may appear in addenda at the end of the volume. Married women are indexed only under their married name. If you do not find the entry you want in the year of death, check the subsequent years

6.25 Each entry gives the name and designation of the deceased, the date and place of death, whether testate or intestate, where and when confirmation was granted, the name and designation of the executor and the value of the estate. If the deceased was testate, we are given the date of the will and the court books in which it has been recorded and when. To investigate further, note the name of the sheriff court where confirmation was granted (which is in heavier type), the date of confirmation, and, if there is a will, in which court books and when it was recorded.

6.26 For example, if you look up 'HARDIE, James Kier, M.P.' in the *Calendar of Conformations and Inventories* for 1915, you find that confirmation to his wife and daughter as executors was granted at AYR on 28 December and that his will was recorded in the court books of the commissariot of Ayr on 27 December. You therefore look at the SC.6 (Ayr sheriff court) repertory. You find that the confirmation of his executors is in a volume referenced SC.6/48/56, but you are more likely to want to see his inventory and will. The Register of Inventories is SC.6/44 and the volume which covers December 1915 is SC.6/44/77, while the Register of Testamentary Writings is SC.6/46 and the volume including December 1915 is SC.6/46/42. Both of these are arranged chronologically and you will find the inventory and will each recorded under the date 27 December 1915, ie they had to be recorded before confirmation was granted.

Wills Elsewhere

6.27 If you have been unable to find a record of your ancestor's executry in the Commissary Court and Sheriff Court commissary records, there are other sources you can try.

6.28 RH.9/8 is a collection of miscellaneous executry papers, 1481–1882. The repertory thereof consists of an index (extended from one published by the Scottish Record Society in 1904). You order by the reference RH.9/8, the date of the document and the name of the deceased.

6.29 If your ancestor was connected with a family whose records have been gifted to or deposited in the SRO, then a copy of his testament may survive among the records of that GD (see 4.18).

6.30 Many wills are registered in the various registers of deeds, which are described in 10.2–16. As explained there, not all of these are indexed and therefore easy to search. What is loosely termed as a 'will' may appear under different names, 'Latter Will and Testament', 'Deed of Settlement', 'Trust Disposition and Settlement', 'Mutual Disposition and Settlement', etc. Dispositions and settlements were often used to get round the rule that heritable property could not be bequeathed. Wills thus registered are likely to be those of better-off folk and of course none should be registered till after the death of the testator. An example of a will in a register of deeds is given in 6.21.

Death Duties

6.31 Connected with the records of executries are estate duty records (IRS. 5–14). These may not give any genealogical information other than what you can obtain from the commissary and sheriff court records, which you should investigate first.

6.32 The estate duty records are part of the records of the Inland Revenue in Scotland and commence in 1804. Look first at the detailed explanation on 'Estate Duty Office Registers' contained in the IRS repertory. There are various series of books and registers, relating to the various taxes which have been levied on the estates of deceased persons. There is a 75-year closure on these records. The categories of estate duty register and the useful non-financial information you might find in them are as follows. The indexes usually give only the relevant folio, and the relevant volume has to be discovered from a study of the IRS repertory.

- IRS.5 Personal Legacy Registers, 1804–1829. These state the relationship of the legatees to the deceased, though not always very specifically, eg 'Mrs Amelia Farquharson, descend^t of Brother of mother' (IRS.5/3).
- IRS.6 Return Ledgers for Inventory Duty, 1831–1892, which account for repayments when there has been over-payments. Date of death. May give name of lawyer.
- IRS.7 Residue Duty Account Books, 1819–1838, account for payments of inventory duty. Name of executor. Indexes, 1808–1850 and 1885–1897, which are indexes to the inventories which are numbered.
- IRS.8 Legacy Receipt Books, 1796–1865. Relationship of legatees.
- IRS.9 Register of Inventories received from Commissary offices, 1824–1876. Indexes, 1863–1884.
- IRS.10 Testate Register and Indexes, 1828–1879. Date of death, executor, relationship of legatees.
- IRS.11 Intestate Register and Indexes, 1829–1879. Executor. Persons beneficially entitled and their relationship. Solicitors.

- IRS.12 Succession Duty Register and Indexes, 1853-1868. Date of death. This record relates to succession in heritable subjects (ie land and houses mainly) which could not be transferred by an ordinary will until 1868. The entries explain why the named successor is succeeding to the heritable property, whether by a legal document or in right of a relationship.

- IRS.13 General Registers, 1880-1906. Date of death. Relationship of beneficiaries.

- IRS.14 Indexes, 1870-1907, to IRS.10, 11, 12 and 13. Date of death. Closed for only 30 years.

7

$\mathcal{J}$nheritance: Heirs in Heritage

7.1 This chapter is concerned with the records of inheritance of heritable property. Clearly, this will matter to you only if your ancestor was likely to have owned his own house or land. Most Scotsmen did not.

7.2 The system of land-holding in Scotland is a feudal one. In theory, almost all land belongs to the Crown, but the Crown grants the effective ownership of land to Crown vassals, who, as subject-superiors, then may grant ownership to their vassals, retaining certain rights. The need of the heir of a deceased vassal to prove his right to inherit, created records which are useful to the ancestor searcher. However, the death of a vassal did not inevitably or immediately result in such a record. Often, the heir simply occupied the lands and did not go through the correct procedures for years. A landowner in his lifetime might dispone lands to his eldest son, reserving a liferent from his property. After 1868, heritable property could be bequeathed. However, whether an heir acquired a property by disposition or by inheritance or by bequest, any such transference of ownership should after 1617 be recorded in the Register of Sasines, where you should also look (see 8.3–18).

7.3 Where there had been no disposition or bequest by a deceased owner of heritage, until 1964 the law of primogeniture applied, by which the eldest son inherited all the heritage, excluding his siblings. If there were no sons but there were daughters, all the daughters inherited equally.

Retours (Services of Heirs)

7.4 The most accessible record of heirs in heritage is the record of Retours, which are part of the Chancery records (C). When a vassal of the Crown died, his heir had to prove his right to inherit his ancestor's lands by the procedure of an inquest and 'retour' (= return) to Chancery. Retours could also be used by less exalted folk to provide evidence of their right to the heritable property of an ancestor. Retours which specified the lands were called special retours. General retours did not name any lands. These special and general retours, which are also known as services of heirs, will tell you the names of the heir and the ancestor, their relationship and sometimes the date of death of the ancestor.

7.5 The retour procedure was also used to appoint a tutor to administer the affairs of a fatherless child (a 'pupil', under 14 if a boy, 12 if a girl). The tutor was usually the nearest adult male relative of the father.

7.6 The retours date from 1530 and are in Latin until 1847 (excepting the years 1652-1659). They are indexed throughout but the style of indexes changes dramatically after 1700. The year 1700 is covered in both series of indexes.

Retours before 1700

7.7 A summary of the retours to 1700 was published in 2 volumes in 1811 and an index thereto in a third volume in 1816. The 3 volumes are entitled *Inquisitionum ad Capellam Regis Retornatarum Abbreviatio*. The title on the spines of the volumes in the Historical Search Room is shortened to *Inquisitionum Retornatarum Abbreviatio*. The summaries and indexes of the special retours are arranged separately within counties. Look in volume 3 under the county in which your ancestor owned land. Under each county, there is an index of names ('Index Nominum') and an index of places ('Index Locorum'). Also look under the headings 'Inquisitiones Generales' and 'Inquisitiones de Tutela' at the 'Index Nominum' of each. Heir, ancestor, tutor and pupil are all indexed.

7.8 An awkwardness in using these indexes is that names are printed as they appear in the original document, the Christian names in their Latin form, and the surnames in variant spellings (eg 'Garden' may appear as 'Gairdin') and therefore not in the form or order you might expect.

7.9 In each index, each name is followed by a number. This number is the running number of the summaries. You then go to volume 1 or 2 and look up that number under the particular county within the 'Inquisitiones Speciales', or under the 'Inquisitiones Generales' or under the 'Inquisitiones de Tutela', depending on the index in which you have found the number. If the entries in a county within the 'Inquisitiones Speciales' seem not to go up to the number you have, then look at the supplementary pages in volume 2 which follow the entries for Wigton.

7.10 Most summaries are in Latin. Each summary is headed by its date, then you get the name of the heir, the name of the ancestor, and the relationship, and in the 'Inquisitiones Speciales' the lands. The date of death is not given, though it may appear in the original record of special retours. In the 'Inquisitiones de Tutela', the first name is that of the tutor, followed by his relationship to his 'pupil' (the child), whose name follows. At the end of each summary, you will find a roman number (= the volume number) and an arabic number (= the folio number) or you will find a letter of the alphabet followed by an arabic number. If you want to see the full document in the Chancery records, you order by the reference C.22 and the volume number, converting that number into an arabic one. The letter references, A to I represent volumes now numbered c.22/177-185 (look at the c repertory for the details). Thus, if the reference is G.172, you order out c.22/183 and, having obtained that volume, look up folio 172.

7.11   If you have failed to find your ancestor in the *Inquisitionum Retornatarum Abbreviatio*, then look at the very end of the Historical Search Room copy of volume II, where you will find four inserted pages, printed in 1900, containing abridgements, in the same format but arranged alphabetically by name of heir, of a few retours from 1303 to 1622 omitted from the official register, but rescued by a Mr Alexander Macdonald. To read the full text of these retours, you order out c.39/4 (a volume of transcripts). The number at the end of each abridgement is the folio number in that volume.

7.12   As there was no time limit for recording retours, some pre-1700 retours were recorded after 1700, occasionally well after.

Retours from 1700

7.13   Starting in 1700 and up to the present day, there is a series of printed 'Indexes to the Services of Heirs in Scotland', decennial up to 1859, annual thereafter, with the title 'Services of Heirs' on the spine. There is more than one decennial or annual index in each volume. These are indexes to the general and special retours, but they do not index the appointments of tutors. Before using these indexes for the first time, you should read the 'explanations' which introduce the volume for 1700-1749.

7.14   These indexes index by name of the heir ('the Person Served') not the ancestor, but at the end of each volume or ten-year period there is a supplement which lists alphabetically the names of ancestors ('Persons Served to') whose heirs do not have the same surname, cross-referring to the names of the heirs. In the index, after the name of the heir, you will find 'distinguishing particulars', ie the heir's designation, the relationship and name of the ancestor, sometimes the latter's date of death, what type of heir, the lands if he is heir special, and the date of the retour. There follows the date of recording and a monthly number: note both of these if you are to proceed further.

7.15   To obtain the call number of the service of heir itself, you must look in the c repertory under c.22 up to 15 November 1847 and after that date under c.28. Choose the volume which includes the date of recording you have found in the index. In that volume, look for the date of recording and the monthly running number, both of which will appear in the margin of the text.

7.16   For example, say you are interested in James Duncan, son of John Duncan, minister in Zetland [Shetland], who in 1736 was served heir to his uncle Henry Robertson, apothecary in Edinburgh. The index tells you that the date of recording was 1736 November 24 and the monthly number is 14. The repertory tells you that the volume for that date is c.22/64. The entries in the volume are in chronological order and you read in the margin 'No 14 of Novr. 1736' beside the copy of the retour, which explains in detail the relationship between the deceased and his heir.

7.17 The date of death of the ancestor is sometimes stated, but more often is not. In the simpler entries of sons succeeding fathers, there may be no additional information in the text (in Latin until 1847) than there is in the index (in English).

7.18 If you are looking for a service of heir between 1700 and 1796 and cannot find it in the 'Services of Heirs' in its proper place, try the one-page 'List of Unrecorded Retours' which is placed in Volume 5 of the 'Services of Heirs' between 1905 and 1906. Those listed which start with the letters A-J will be found by ordering out C.25/10 and with letters L-Y in C.25/11.

7.19 If you are looking for a service of heir between 1792 and 1846 and cannot find it in the 'Services of Heirs', try the 'Index of Retours of General Service', which were dated before 1847 but recorded after 1859. This index is also placed in Volume 5 of the 'Services of Heirs' between 1905 and 1906. You will find these retours either in C.22/175 or 176, depending on the date of recording.

7.20 If you are looking for the retour of the appointment of a tutor to administer the affairs of a child, there is a typed index covering the period 1701-1886 (which index also covers the appointment of curators to administer the affairs of insane persons until 1897). The index is by name of the child and gives the volume and folio numbers of the record. Order by the reference C.22 and the volume number. There are no such retours after 1886, as this method of administering the affairs of a child had fallen into disuse, having gradually been replaced by an alternative method, that of the appointment of a factor loco tutoris by the Court of Session (see 11.23), or, after 1880, by a sheriff court if the estate was small (see 11.36-41).

Inquests

7.21 The decision that someone was indeed the heir of a deceased person or the right person to be tutor to a fatherless child was made locally by an inquest. The decision of the inquest was then 'retoured' to Chancery. At the beginning of every retour, we are told in which sheriff or burgh court the inquest was held. Sometimes, but only sometimes, the sheriff court preserved the records of the inquest and these records may provide further family details (and are in English). For example, in the Register of Retours we are told simply that, in 1844, Thomas Crocket, plasterer in Dumfries, was served heir to his great-grandfather, Andrew Thomson, slater in Dumfries (C.22/166). The equivalent sheriff court records provide the names of Thomas's parents, grandparents and a great-aunt (SC.15/64/2). To find if the required sheriff court records have survived, look in the contents list of the relevant SC repertory for 'Services of Heirs' or 'Record of Services' or similar headings.

Those of Jedburgh sheriff court are calendared and indexed in *Services of Heirs, Roxburghshire* (Scottish Record Society). Inquests held in a burgh court may be recorded in the burgh court book (see 11.48). Unless the inquest decision was not retoured, this source is unlikely to provide additional details to those in the retours, but will be in English.

Clare Constat

7.22 The heir of a crown vassal had to have a special retour before he could inherit his ancestor's lands. An heir, whose deceased ancestor was the feudal vassal of a subject-superior, might obtain a document called a precept of clare constat from that superior before he could legally own his ancestor's lands. In this document (usually in Latin), the superior acknowledged that it clearly appeared to him that the heir was the heir of a deceased vassal in specified lands. A precept of clare constat will tell you who the heir and ancestor were, and their relationship. There is no register of such documents, but some survive in private collections (GDs, see 4.18-19), while the instruments of sasine, which followed both them and special retours and repeated the information therein, may be found both in GD collections and in the Register of Sasines (RS – see 8.3-18).

Tailzies

7.23 In the Services of Heirs, you may have noticed that an heir may be served as 'Heir of Taillie'. 'Taillie' or 'tailzie' is the Scots form of the word 'entail'. By an Act of the Scottish Parliament 1685, c.22, a land owner was allowed to decide who would succeed to his heritable estate for generations to come by means of a deed of tailzie. Such a deed had to be recorded in the Register of Tailzies (RT.1) and, in the naming of a series of substitute heirs, may include detailed information about the family at that time. For example, in the deed of entail by Major Charles Hamilton of Fairholm, recorded in 1777 (RT.1/19, f.265), he names as his heirs, in order, his natural son, a cousin german [first cousin on father's side] another cousin german, his natural daughter, and then six other cousins. Remember that an heir of tailzie usually had to take the surname of the entailer along with the lands, and therefore might have to change his name.

7.24 There is an index to the Register of Tailzies between 1688, when the Register starts, and 1833. This index is a mixture of print and manuscript and lists the granters of the deeds, arranged chronologically under each surname letter. You order by the reference RT.1 and the volume number given in the index, which also gives the folio number. The names of the heirs often appear well into a rather lengthy document.

7.25 A digest of the Register of Tailzies between 1688 and 1810, in the Historical Search Room, is of little use as it omits the names of the heirs.

7.26 If you are looking for an entry in the Register of Tailzies after 1833, you should go to the Legal Search Room to consult a 2-volume manuscript index, referenced RT.3/1/1-2. This indexes the period 1688-1938. Again, the arrangement is alphabetical by first letter of the surname only, then chronological. At the end of each entry, there is a volume and folio number: eg if the entry concludes '114-275', then you order RT.1/114 and look up folio 275 therein. Since 1914, the Register contains only disentails.

Beneficium Inventarii

7.27 Until 1847, an heir who took over an ancestor's heritable property could be liable for all the ancestor's debts. However, by an Act of 1695, c.24, an heir who entered by the procedure 'cum beneficio inventarii' was liable only to the extent of the value of the heritable property, provided it was done within a year and a day of the ancestor's death. This procedure is recorded in the Register of Inventories of Heirs Entering Cum Beneficio Inventarii (RD.20), which dates from 1696 to 1850. This register is not indexed. A list of the volumes in the Register and the dates they cover is in the RD repertory. The name of a party is put in the margin at the start of each entry, but this may be the name of either the heir or of the ancestor. You will find in each 'inventory' the names of the heir and his deceased ancestor, sometimes the date of death, and an inventory of the heritable property and the income therefrom.

7.28 The lack of an index limits the usefulness of this record, but there is information in it. Heirs may be cousins. The heirs are not necessarily well-to-do. In 1826, James Davidson, labourer in the parish of Ardclach, was heir to his brother David Davidson, vintner in Nairn (RD.20/14, f.153). The next entry in the same volume illustrates how far Scotsmen travelled - Robert Walkinshaw, 'at present in Mexico', was heir to his brother William Walkinshaw, captain in the service of the Honourable East India Company, who died at Ghazapore in the East Indies (RD.20/14, f.156).

7.29 Another record which contains information about heirs who were liable for their ancestor's debts is the Register of Adjudications. (See 11.59-61.)

Ultimus Haeres

7.30 Perhaps you are seeking an ancestor who was believed to have died without a known heir. In such a case, the Crown would be the ultimus haeres (last heir) and the heritable and moveable property of the deceased would have been paid into the Exchequer, any lands being sold or granted to a new owner. Fortune hunters should be warned that almost all ultimus haeres estates comprise small amounts of money and that such estates are usually distributed to people who have a moral claim, though not a legal one, such as a relative by marriage who cared for the deceased in his old age. Such claimants would petition for a share of the estate.

7.31 Obviously, you must know the name of the deceased and the approximate date of death.

7.32 Because of legal limitations in the past on those who might succeed on intestacy, the Ultimus Haeres records contain more genealogical information than you might expect. Such limitations were:

a.   If a man died childless and intestate, but left a widow, she could claim only part of the estate.

b.   A bastard could be succeeded in both heritable and moveable property only by the offspring of his own body. Until 1836, if a bastard had no children, he could not bequeath any property to anyone, unless he had received letters of legitimation from the Crown.

c.   There was no succession to or through the mother in either heritable or moveable property, ie if a person died intestate and childless, with no relations on his father's side, but with relations on his mother's side including half-brothers or -sisters, they were excluded and all his property went to the Crown as ultimus haeres. (Since 1855, there has been gradual reform in this legal area.) Thus, many of the petitioners for a gift of an ultimus haeres estate were maternal relations of the deceased and their petitions contain much information about their families.

7.33 Ultimus Haeres records change dramatically in 1834.

Ultimus Haeres before 1834

7.34 Records before 1834 relate almost entirely to the granting of ultimus haeres property to petitioners. Such grants of moveable property were made under the Privy Seal (see 5.17). Those up to 1584 will be found in the printed volumes of the *Register of the Privy Seal*, in which both the deceased and the donee are indexed. Between 1585 and 1660, you must use the minute books (PS.6) to search for such a grant. The originals are ordered by PS.1 and the volume number. From 1660, there are two indexes, but only the index from 1782 identifies the gifts of ultimus haeres, indexing both the donees and estates. Order by the reference PS.3 and the volume number. The record of grants of heritable property exists only for the periods 1750-1761 and from 1831 and is unindexed: see the c.14 repertory.

7.35 Petitions for grants of ultimus haeres are preserved among the Exchequer records (E.303). The accompanying papers usually include a report advising whether or not a grant should be made. These records are incomplete and unindexed. If you wish to investigate them, look at the list of E.303 in the Exchequer repertory. Some do give detailed family information, eg the papers in the case in 1797 of Lt Col John Rose, a bastard who died in Corsica, demonstrate his relationship to a number of people in the Nairn area, including a minister and a bailie, as well as a bricklayer in Glasgow and a book-keeper in Jamaica (E.303/6).

Ultimus Haeres from 1834

7.36 The present procedure for dealing with ultimus haeres cases dates from 1834 and from then there are consistent records. These are in various series which are explained in the repertory (E.851-870). There is no overall index, but each individual volume is indexed by name of the deceased person, giving the surname and christian name only.

7.37 To search, firstly you want to check if the estate of someone you are researching did fall to the Crown. Look at the indexes in the Procedure Books (E.851), which give a summary of proceedings relating to every case. Some of these books have two indexes (a separate one for bastards). Alternatively, from 1886 you can look at annual alphabetical lists (E.869). Once you have established that there was an ultimus haeres case of interest to you, you can look it up in a relevant volume or file of the other series. Particularly useful are the Treasury Reports (E.853) which repeat the claims of the petitioners and often include detailed family relationships and histories.

Relations of Lt Col John Rose, 1797. (E.303/6)

8

Owners of Land and Houses

8.1 The previous chapter concerned the transfer of heritable property when the owner died. The ownership, and transfer of ownership, of land and houses is of such importance that records thereof are among the earliest to survive. The system of land-holding in Scotland is a feudal one. In a feudal system, all land is held of the Crown, either directly or through a subject-superior.

8.2 A grant of land was usually made in a charter by the Crown or subject-superior, but used to require a series of legal documents. You will find examples of the more important ones, which were often in Latin, in Gouldesbrough's *Formulary of Old Scots Legal Documents* (Stair Society). The most important was the instrument of sasine, which until 1858 finalised all grants of land (including Crown ones) and was essential evidence that change of ownership had taken place. From 1617, such instruments were copied into the Register of Sasines, which is the primary source of information of ownership of property.

Register of Sasines

8.3 Whenever heritable property changed hands or was used as security for a loan, then the document narrating the legal transaction should be copied ('recorded') in the Register of Sasines. The Register was founded in 1617, though there had been a trial run between 1599 and 1609 called the Secretary's Register, and continues to the present day, when it is being replaced by registration of title. The Secretary's Register is now treated as part of the Register of Sasines and therefore will not be dealt with separately.

8.4 We talk of the Register of Sasines, but in fact there are several registers of sasines. The Secretary's Register was kept in various divisions of the country. Between 1617 and 1868, there was a General Register of Sasines, in which could be recorded documents relating to property in any part of Scotland, and Particular Registers, each for a particular area of the country. Since then, there has been a separate division of the Register for each county. There were separate registers for property in the royal burghs (see 8.16-18).

8.5 The Register of Sasines is particularly useful to genealogists, both because fathers often made gifts of land to their children, and because a document narrating the sale or mortgage of lands may tell you the designation of the granter when he acquired the lands. Therefore you can trace in the Register the development both of families and individuals. Documents therein often refer back to earlier transactions and thus may name persons who died prior to the date of the document.

8.6 After 1780, the Register of Sasines is quite easy to search: before that date, less so.

Register of Sasines 1617-1780

8.7 First, you should know in which part of Scotland your ancestor may have owned land. Unless the property lies within a royal burgh, you should next search the relevant Particular Register. There is a series of indexes but it is an incomplete series. The following table gives the modern county and the equivalent Particular Register and says whether there is a pre-1780 index therefor. The indexes marked with an asterisk have been published, may be purchased from the SRO and should be available through a library.

County	Particular Register of Sasines	Indexes
Aberdeen	Aberdeen till 1660 (RS.4-5) Aberdeen and Kincardine from 1661 (RS.8)	1599-1660*
Angus (Forfar)	Forfar (RS.33-35)	1620-1700* 1701-1780
Argyll	Argyll etc (RS.9-10)	1617-1780*
Ayr	Ayr etc (RS.11-14)	1599-1660*
Banff	Banff (RS.15-17)	1600-1780*
Berwick	Berwick etc (RS.18-19)	1617-1780*
Bute	Argyll etc (RS.9-10)	1617-1780*
Caithness	Inverness till 1644 (RS.36-37) Caithness from 1646 (RS.20-21)	1606-1780*
Clackmannan	Stirling etc (RS.58-59)	None
Dumfries	Dumfries etc (RS.22-23)	1617-1780*
Dunbarton	Argyll etc (RS.9-10)	1617-1780*
East Lothian (Haddington)	Edinburgh etc (RS.24-27)	1599-1660* 1741-1780
Edinburgh city	Edinburgh etc (RS.24-27)	1599-1660* 1741-1780
Fife	Fife and Kinross till 1685 Fife from 1685 (RS.30-32)	1603-1660*
Glasgow city	Renfrew and Glasgow (RS.53-54)	None
Inverness	Inverness etc (RS.36-38)	1606 1780*
Kincardine	Kincardine till 1657 Aberdeen and Kincardine from 1661 (RS.6-8)	1600-1657*

County	Particular Register of Sasines	Indexes
Kinross	Fife and Kinross till 1685	1603–1660★
	Kinross from 1688 (RS.30–31, 39)	
Kirkcudbright	Dumfries etc (RS.22–23)	1617–1780★
Lanark	Lanark (RS.40–42)	1618–1780★
Midlothian	Edinburgh etc (RS.24–27)	1599–1660★
(Edinburgh)		1741–1780
Moray (Elgin)	Elgin and Nairn (RS.28–29)	1617–1780★
Nairn	Elgin and Nairn (RS.28–29)	1617–1780★
Orkney	Orkney and Shetland (RS.43–47)	1617–1660
Peebles	Roxburgh etc (RS.55–57)	None
Perth	Perth (RS.48–52)	1601–1609
	Stirling etc (RS.58–59)	None
Renfrew	Renfrew and Glasgow (RS.53–54)	None
Ross and Cromarty	Inverness etc (RS.36–38)	1606–1780★
Roxburgh	Roxburgh etc (RS.55–57)	None
Selkirk	Roxburgh etc (RS.55–57)	None
Shetland	Orkney and Shetland (RS.43–47)	1617–1660
Stirling	Stirling etc (RS.58–59)	None
Sutherland	Inverness etc (RS.36–38)	1606–1780★
West Lothian	Edinburgh etc (RS.24–27)	1599–1660★
(Linlithgow)		1700–1780
Wigtown	Wigtown (RS.60–61)	None

8.8 Determine which Particular Register is the likely one to include your ancestor. If there is an index for that PRS and for that period, obviously you look up that index. These indexes were compiled over several decades and vary in style, but will give the volume and commencing folio for each document in which your ancestor appears. All parties who are mentioned as having or having had a heritable right (ie not tenants) in the property should be indexed, not just the main parties in the transaction. In some indexes, the volume will be expressed in roman numerals and you will have to convert that into its arabic form. You order by the RS reference number and the volume number, eg RS.29/7. Because most of the indexes were compiled before the reference number system was introduced, the RS reference number will not be in the index, but it has usually been annotated at the start of the index. If in doubt check the RS repertory.

8.9 If there is no index for that Particular Register or period, then look at the RS repertory for the minute books of that Register. The starting dates of these minute books vary considerably. If there is a minute book for the relevant period, you must order it out by its call number like any other document. The minute books are arranged chronologically by the date of recording. Each minute also states the names of the main parties and lands, and the relevant folios in the volume of the Register. The volume number may not be apparent and should be ascertained, along with its call number, by its dates, from the repertory.

8.10 If there is no minute book nor index, you have no alternative but to browse through the volumes of the Register itself, which can be a formidable task.

8.11 As the majority of documents in the Register are instruments of sasine, you should familiarise yourself with the structure of this type of deed. Gouldesbrough's *Formulary* contains examples in Latin with English translations. If you are lucky, the copy in the Register will start with an introduction which will tell you to whom the lands were granted, or his name will appear in the margin. In the instrument itself, the first name to be mentioned should be either the grantee or his legal agent. The granter may also have a legal agent (called a 'bailie'). In other words, you must read the document carefully to disentangle who is doing what. In genealogical terms, an added advantage is that witnesses were often relations of the parties. There are two lists of witnesses in an instrument of sasine, one near the end and one about two-thirds through the document at the end of what was known as the precept of sasine.

8.12 As well as searching for your ancestor in the Particular Register for the area in which he owned land, you should also look in the General Register of Sasines, which is indexed up to 1720. From then to 1780, you have to use the minute books which you will find listed in the RS repertory under the reference number RS.62.

Register of Sasines after 1780

8.13 Firstly, decide in which county your ancestor may have owned land. Next, go to the volumes which are stored in the stairwell beneath the stairs which lead to the Historical Search Room. These volumes are the Sasine Abridgements and indexes thereto. These Abridgements contain printed summaries of all the documents recorded in the Register of Sasines from 1781, chronologically within counties. They are indexed by persons from 1781 to the present and by places from 1781 to 1830 and from 1872 to the present. The earlier abridgements are kept in blocks of years, but more recently each year is separate.

8.14 Select the volume of Abridgements you want for the county and year(s) in which you are interested. Select the equivalent index of persons, which will be in a separate volume. Make sure it is the equivalent index: the covering dates are usually at the top of each page. Look up your ancestor's name in the index of persons, which gives simply the surname and Christian name, no designation. After the name you will find a number or series of numbers. These numbers are the running numbers of the summaries in the Abridgements. Find the summary which starts with that number. It will be headed by a date and then will tell you, *inter alia*, the names and designations of the new and previous owners and a description of the property. All parties are indexed. If your ancestor's name is a common one and you know the name of the property he owned, you might wish to look up the index of places as well as that of persons to see if any of the summary numbers coincide.

(824)   Jan. 3. 1812.
JOSEPH COOK, Shoemaker, College of Elgin, *Seised*, Dec.
31. 1811,—in lands called SPYNIE MANSE in the COL-
LEGE OF ELGIN;—on Disp. by John Harral, Gardener,
College of Elgin, to Isobel Adam, his spouse, in liferent, and
Margaret, Katharine, Janet, Christian, and Isobel Mathew,
daughters of Alexander Mathew in Cloves, in fee, Jun. 27.
1786; and Disp. & Assig. by them, Dec. 26. 27. 1811.
                                        P. R. 10. 49.

(825)   Jan. 13. 1812.
JOHN COULL, Gardener, Elgin, & Ann Stewart, his spouse,
—and James Coull, their son, *Seised*, in liferent & fee respectively, Jan. 13. 1812,—in part of the south end of that Habita-
tion Manse or Messuage commonly called the MANSE OF
KINNORE with the Houses thereon, on the south side of the
Cathedral Church of Moray and on the west of the Vennel
called Niddry's wynd within the COLLEGE OF ELGIN;—on
Disp. by Alexander Shiach, Cartwright, Elgin, Nov. 21. 1811.
                                        P. R. 10. 53.

(826)   Jan. 13. 1812.
JANET WILLIAMSON, relict of James Lillie, Butcher,
Forres, *Seised*, Dec. 31. 1811,—in 2 Ridges of land consisting
of 1 Acre in the middle of the MUIRYSHADE; & 9 Ridges
of land on the west side of the said Muiryshade consisting of
3 Acres & 1 rood, all in the neighbourhood of FORRES;—in
security of a liferent annuity of £10;—on Bond by John Lillie,
Merchant. Forres, Jul. 10. 1810.   P. R. 10. 57.

(827)   Jan. 28. 1812.
WILLIAM TOD, Factor for the Duke of Gordon at Fochabers, *gets Ren.* Oct. 17. 1808,—Dec. 2. 1811, by Jean Grant,
relict of Alexander Smith, Vintner, Fochabers, Edward Smith
at Slave Lake, North America, George Smith at Pictou, Pro-
vince of Nova Scotia, & Isobel Smith, & William Reid, Merchant, Mill of Fochabers, her husband,—of 2 Tenements of
ground with the Houses thereon on the south side of the principal Street called Gordon's Street of FOCHABERS, par.
Bellie;—and of £200, in Disp. by the said Jean Grant, May
18. 1793.   P. R. 10. 62.

(828)   Feb. 15. 1812.
JOHN FORBES, Advocate, *Seised*, Feb. 15. 1812,—in
SCOTSTOWNHILL, par. St. Andrews;—on Ch. Resig.
G. S. Feb. 3. 1812.   P. R. 10. 76.

(829)   Feb. 15. 1812.
JOHN FORBES, Advocate, *Seised*, Feb. 15. 1812,—in
SCOTSTOWNHILL, and Teinds, par. St. Andrews;—on
Disp. by John Innes of Blackhills, to Lieut.-Col. Alexander
Penrose Cumming Gordon of Altyre & Gordonstown, Nov. 24.
1795; Disp. and Assig. by him, to John Penrose Cumming,
Fellow of the New College of Oxford, Dec. 3. 1795; Ret. Sp.
Serv. of Sir William Gordon Cumming Gordon of Altyre &

Excerpt from Sasine Abridgements for Elgin and Forres.

8.15 The summary in the Abridgements may give you all the information you require, but if you wish to study the full text of the document in the Register of Sasines, take note of the numbers given at the end of the summary. You will then have to go back to the Historical Search Room to find the call numbers from the RS repertory and to order out the Sasine volume. If the number at the end of the summary is preceded by the letters GR, then the document will be in the General Register of Sasines (RS.3); if by the letters PR, then it will be in the Particular Register of Sasines which includes that county (see list at 8.7); and if it is preceded by no letters, then it will be in one of the post-1868 county divisions of the Register. As usual the first number is the volume number, and the second number the folio number, and you order by the RS number and the volume number. For example, a Clackmannan abridgement dated 'Dec. 28, 1802' ends 'PR.37.333'. The Particular Register of Sasines for Stirling and Clackmannan is RS.59 and you order out RS.59/37. A Glasgow abridgement in 1881 ends with the reference '1064.174'. You find from the list in the RS repertory that the Glasgow call number is RS.102 and order out RS.102/1064.

Burgh Registers of Sasines

8.16 Each royal burgh was entitled to have its own burgh register of sasines. If your ancestor owned property in a royal burgh, then the record of that ownership will probably not be in the General or a Particular Register of Sasines, though it is wise to check them as well as the burgh register. Remember that many of these burghs lay within much smaller boundaries than they do today. The SRO holds the registers of sasines of the burghs of Aberdeen, Annan★, Anstruther Wester, Arbroath, Auchtermuchty★, Ayr, Banff, Brechin, Burntisland★, Crail, Cullen★, Culross★, Cupar, Dingwall, Dornoch, Dumbarton, Dumfries, Dunbar, Dundee, Dunfermline, Dysart★, Earlsferry, Edinburgh★, Elgin, Falkland, Forfar★, Forres, Fortrose★, Haddington, Hawick, Inverbervie★, Inverkeithing, Inverness, Inverurie, Irvine, Jedburgh, Kinghorn★, Kintore★, Kirkcaldy★, Kirkcudbright, Kirkwall, Lanark, Lauder, Linlithgow, Lochmaben★, Montrose, Nairn★, Newburgh★, New Galloway, North Berwick★, Paisley★, Peebles, Perth, Pittenweem, Queensferry★, Renfrew, Rothesay, Rutherglen, St Andrews, Sanquhar, Selkirk, Stirling, Stranraer, Tain★, Whithorn★, Wigtown★. The Glasgow burgh register and the Aberdeen and Dundee pre-1809 registers are kept by Glasgow City Archives, Aberdeen City Archives and City of Dundee Archive and Record Centre respectively (addresses in Appendix A).

8.17 The commencement dates of the Burgh Registers of Sasines held by the SRO vary tremendously from 1602 (Dysart) to 1881 (Forres). They were discontinued at various dates between 1926 and 1963 and thereafter all properties appear in the General Register of Sasines. The burgh registers marked with an asterisk in 8.16 have typescript indexes, but none of these start before 1809 and they index only those who are being granted ownership. If your ancestor lived in one of the asterisked burghs after 1809, look up the relevant index. Each index entry gives a volume and folio number, but to find the call number, you have to consult the burgh repertory (B), eg in the index to the Burgh Register of Sasines of Whithorn, there is an entry for Peter Houl, soldier in 7th Hussars, in 1815. The volume is 1, the folio 100, and you order out B.71/2/1 and look up folio 100. As Whithorn, like most burghs, has more than one series of its Register of Sasines, you must make certain by checking the date that you are ordering the volume from the correct series.

8.18   To search for your ancestor otherwise in a Burgh Register of Sasines, look up the introduction to the Burgh repertory (B) to find the number that relates to that particular burgh (eg Culross is B.12). Look up the pages under that number to find the dates of that Burgh Register. Check to see if there is a manuscript index or minute book, which you may consult. If there is not, you will have to go directly to a volume of the Burgh Register of Sasines, some of which have a contents list or index in the volume.

Notarial Protocol Books

8.19   If you are seeking an ancestor who owned heritable property before the setting up of the Register of Sasines in 1617 or before the start of the burgh registers of sasines or if you cannot find an entry in the Register of Sasines before 1660, you might investigate the Notarial Protocol books. These were record books kept by notaries, who were lawyers officially authorised to draw up certain legal documents, including instruments of sasine. Their books contain copies or notes of the documents they compiled. Not all these books were kept to the standard one might expect in a public register.

8.20   If your ancestor owned property in a royal burgh (see 8.16), look up the B repertory at the list of records under the name of that burgh to see if they include any protocol books (not all do). There you will find the reference number and covering dates of each protocol book. A handful are indexed, but most are not, and therefore you must simply order out the book which covers the approximate date and browse through it.

8.21   If your ancestor owned property anywhere else, go to the repertory of Notarial records (NP). This includes a topographical guide, mainly under the names of counties, which will provide you with the reference numbers of the books of notaries who worked in that part of Scotland: eg if you look up Shetland, you will find only one notary who operated there between 1576 and 1615, the reference number of his protocol book being NP.1/36. None of these books is indexed, but the repertory notes those which have been printed by the Scottish Record Society and those for which there are abstracts. These abstracts are referenced RH.2/1/16-26 (see the RH.2 repertory). You may find the abstracts and printed versions, both of which are translated into English, easier to read than the originals, and the printed books are indexed.

Crown Grants of Land

8.22   If you think your ancestor was granted lands by a Crown charter, there are three other records you should examine - those of the Great Seal, Privy Seal and Signatures. The copies of charters in the Register of the Privy Seal and the Signatures were, in effect, drafts of those in the Great Seal Register. The Signatures have the advantage that they are in English while the Great and Privy Seal records are in Latin. It is suggested that you search first in the Great Seal Register, and then search in the Privy Seal Register or Signatures if the charter is not in the Great Seal register or you require the English version in the Signatures.

Great Seal

8.23 The record of the charters issued under the Great Seal dates from 1314 and is published up to 1668 in the eleven volumes of the *Register of the Great Seal of Scotland (or Registrum Magni Sigilli Regum Scotorum*, or *RMS* for short). As volume 1 of the *RMS* was compiled from a variety of sources and few people are likely to trace their ancestry back to the 14th century, the following comments are to the record from 1424, when volume 2 of the *RMS* starts.

8.24 Each volume of the *RMS* is indexed. The charters (in summary form) and indexes are in Latin until 1651. If you are looking for a Crown charter to your ancestor up to 1668, look up the 'Index Nominum' in the volume of the *RMS* which covers the likely date. In these indexes up to 1651, Christian names are in Latin or are abbreviated and designations are in Latin. Each entry in the index is followed by a number - this is the running number of the summaries in the volume. These summaries are quite detailed, but if you want to see the original, take note of the numbers at the end of the summary, the roman number being the volume number and the arabic the running number (not the folio number) of the charters in the original record.

8.25 If the roman number is preceded by the letters 'PR'(which stands for 'Paper Register') order out by the reference C.3 and the volume number (converted into arabic). Otherwise, the call number is C.2 and the volume number, but, as many of the volumes are in two bulky parts, you should look at the Chancery repertory under c.2 to check which part you should order. For example, in the *RMS*, volume 4, you have found an entry concerning a family named Leslie, and at the end of the entry you read 'xxxiv.582'. If you look in the repertory, you find that volume 34 is in two parts and no. 582 is in the second part; and therefore you should order out C.2/34 part 2.

8.26 If you are seeking your ancestor in this record from 1668, look at the several typed indexes to the various series of Great Seal records. The indexes which deal with grants of lands are a 4-volume index to the Register of the Great Seal itself 1668-1919, an index to the Paper Register 1668-1852 and an index to the Principality Register 1716-1913. The introductory notes to these indexes explain the differences between the records. Each index gives the name and designation of the grantee, the lands granted, the date, and the volume and either folio or running number of the charter in that volume. If the charter is in the Great Seal Register, order by C.2, the volume number and the part number if the volume is in two parts (the repertory will tell you). If it is in the Paper Register, order by c.3 and the volume number. If it is in the Principality Register, check the introduction to the index to find out the call number (mostly c.16) and order by that and the volume number. The Paper Register continues after 1852 but contains no further grants of land.

Privy Seal

8.27 How to search the Privy Seal has been described in 5.17. Use the printed and indexed *Register of the Privy Seal of Scotland* up to 1584, and the minute books thereafter. The call number up to 1660 is PS.1 and the volume number. After 1660, the call number of the 'Latin Register' in which grants of land are recorded is PS.2 and the volume number. The only indexes to PS.2 are a rather variable set of manuscript indexes between 1660 and 1705, which you order out by PS.7/2.

Signatures

8.28 The surviving Signatures date from 1607 to 1847. There is a 2-volume index which tells you the name of the grantee, the lands, the date, and the box and running number or volume and folio number of the signatures. Order by SIG.1 and the box and running number or SIG.2 and the volume number.

Original Charters and Other Writs

8.29 If you have been unable to find a grant of land to your ancestor in the Crown records or registers of sasines or protocol books, you should investigate original documents, particularly before 1660. After that date, the Register of Sasines is complete enough to be reliable.

8.30 The main source for original legal documents in the SRO is the Gifts and Deposits series (see 4.18-19). Check the inventories of GDs which concern likely families or relevant parts of Scotland. A few GDs include cartularies, which list grants given by subject-superiors.

8.31 Other series of original documents may be found in the inventories of the RH class of records. Particularly useful are RH.9/15, which contains miscellaneous writs of lands in Orkney and Shetland, arranged by place-names, and RH.6-8, which contain miscellaneous charters and other writs.

8.32 The writs in RH.6 date between 1142 and 1600. They are calendared in 15 volumes ('Calendar of Charters', on the open shelves) and indexed in 8 volumes. All parties, including witnesses, are indexed. The index gives each personal name and designation and the running number in the calendar. RH.6 has one running number throughout. The entry in the calendar may suffice you and is in English, but if you wish to see the original, order by RH.6 and the running number.

8.33 The writs in RH.7 date from 1601 to 1830. As they are not individually listed, there is no easy way of identifying the persons involved in them, but, as they are arranged in strict chronological order, if you are looking for a writ of a particular date, you can order out the box which includes writs for that year by the reference RH.7 and the box number you find in the repertory.

8.34 The writs in RH.8 are dated between 1700 and 1800 and are arranged by name of the grantee. There is a two-volume inventory. If you wish to see a document, order by RH.8 and the running number in the margin of the inventory.

Valuation Rolls

8.35 Information about the ownership and sometimes tenancy of land and houses was often gathered because of taxes on the value of such properties. From 1855, the Valuation Rolls (VR) themselves supply this information consistently for the whole of Scotland. Prior to that date, records of such information for tax purposes are occasional.

Valuation Rolls before 1855

8.36 Valuation rolls prior to 1855 are sporadic and inconsistent. As the purpose of such a record was to record the value of lands, in some instances that is all that is given and the names of proprietors and occupiers are simply omitted. Still, however imperfect for your purposes these records are, you may wish to take pot luck with them. If you do find the name of a proprietor you are seeking, you may be led on to search a more productive record, such as the Register of Sasines or a GD collection.

8.37 Firstly, look in the part of the Exchequer repertory (E) which includes the reference E.106. Here are listed valuation rolls, arranged by counties and dated variously between 1643 and 1835. Published versions are noted. If you order out a roll, you will discover that it is arranged by parishes. Sometimes no personal names are given; sometimes only the biggest landowners are named, eg 'Robert Arbuthnot of Katerlane for himselff and remnant heritors' (E.106/1/2); but occasionally tenants are named in the description of lands, eg 'That part of Old Mains posest by Jas Forsyth' (E.106/14/2). *A Directory of Land Ownership in Scotland c.1770* by Lorretta R Timperley (Scottish Record Society) is largely based on these valuation rolls for 1771 and is indexed.

8.38 Next, if you are interested in early 19th-century valuation rolls, look at the Inland Revenue repertory (IRS). It lists land tax or valuation rolls for the following counties and dates before 1855. Within counties, the arrangement is by parishes.

       Aberdeen, 1847-57. (IRS.4/1)
       Ayr, c1837-1839. (IRS.4/2)
       Banff, 1836-1837. (IRS.4/3)

Dumfries, 1827. (IRS.4/5)
Fife, 1837. (IRS.4/7)
Lanark, 1837–41 (IRS.3/11) and 1846–60. (IRS.4/8)
Midlothian and Edinburgh city, 1814, 1837–71. (IRS.4/9)
Roxburgh, 1842. (IRS.4/12)
Stirling, 1831. (IRS.4/14)

Again the information supplied varies. You will probably be given the names of the proprietors or most of them. They may be listed alphabetically, showing the parishes in which they owned land. If you are lucky, you may find the names not only of proprietors, but also of tenants who paid land tax. Watch out for later annotations, of unspecified date, which may confuse the information.

8.39 There are some valuation rolls among the Gifts and Deposits. Many can be located using the SRO's Clio textbase. Other GD collections not yet on this system will require more hunting.

8.40 If your ancestor owned property in a royal burgh, then these valuation rolls will not be useful. A separate collection of land tax was made within each royal burgh from the inhabitants thereof. Of the royal burgh records at present within the Scottish Record Office, only Inverkeithing, Jedburgh, Linlithgow, North Berwick and Peebles include cess or stent rolls which list the inhabitants liable to pay tax, prior to 1855. These records sometimes state the trade of the inhabitant, but rarely the property owned. Look them up in the B repertory to find the dates covered and the reference number.

8.41 Similar valuations were made of each parish by the heritors and some survive in the Heritors Records (HR). The heritors were the landowners in each parish who until 1925 were responsible for the maintenance of church, manse, school and (until 1845) the poor of the parish. The money to pay for these outlays was raised from the landowners themselves by assessment on the value of their lands. Records of such assessments survive for a minority of parishes and are mainly 19th century. The heritors are always named in them, their lands not always. If you know the name of the parish in which your ancestor may have owned land, look it up in the index of parishes which is part of the HR repertory. The index will supply the reference number of the parish, eg Dunbar is HR.69. You then look in the repertory at the list of records under that reference number for any assessment rolls or book or lists. (Dunbar has assessment rolls between 1773 and 1904 – HR.69/10/4). As landowners could reclaim from their tenants half of the sum they paid towards poor relief, these assessment rolls very occasionally include the names of tenants with or without the names of their farms. Lands in a royal burgh were usually assessed and paid in a block, without naming the property owners.

8.42 The names of property owners may also be found in the tax records referenced E.326 and 327, discussed in 13.5–11. If your ancestor owned or occupied a property in Midlothian, including Edinburgh, between 1803 and 1812, you should find him in the Property Tax records (E.327/78–121) or Small House or Cottage Tax records (E.327/122–127).

Valuation Rolls since 1855

8.43 The Lands Valuation (Scotland) Act 1854 established a uniform valuation of lands and heritages throughout Scotland. Separate valuation rolls were to be compiled annually for every burgh and county, listing every heritable property, along with the names and designations of the proprietor, tenant and occupier, and its value. However, one proviso, unfortunate from our point of view, was that the occupiers of property which was let at less than £4 per year did not need to be named. With that exception, if your ancestor owned or occupied property in Scotland since 1855, his name should appear in the Valuation Rolls. Only the heads of households would be named.

8.44 Look at the repertory of the Valuation Rolls (VR) for the burgh or county in which you think your ancestor owned or occupied property. The burghs are listed first, then the counties and cities. There is no persons index, but sometimes there are indexes of streets and place-names - these are noted in the repertory. Within the annual volume for a county, the arrangement may be alphabetical by parishes. Ayr county is divided into Carrick, Cunningham and Kyle, but a list of parishes in each of these districts is placed at the start of the list of Ayr county rolls. Lanark county is divided into Upper, Middle and Lower wards.

8.45 Searching for a particular person, even if you know the likely address, can be painstaking. If you are searching in a well-populated part of the country, there may be several volumes for each year through which you have to search. The arrangement within volumes may not always seem logical and is not necessarily consistent year-by-year. The entries for one street will often be dispersed. Street numbers and names can both have been changed over the years.

8.46 Edinburgh and Glasgow VRS are particularly awkward to search. Glasgow, up to 1909, is valued within the parishes of Glasgow, Govan and Barony. An index of streets in 1875-6 is available in the Legal Search Room. As it shows the parish each street is in, it can be used for other years to identify the volume you should order out. Edinburgh is divided by parishes up to 1895, and thereafter by wards. A preliminary study of 19th-century large-scale Ordnance Survey maps and city directories (which give the ward numbers of streets) is recommended, perhaps in combination with a visit to the Edinburgh Room in the Edinburgh Central Library. The Edinburgh Valuation Rolls since 1912 have street indexes which are available in the Legal Search Room.

Electors

8.47 As, until 1918, ownership of heritable property above a certain value was a qualification for the right to vote in a parliamentary election, your land-owning ancestor may appear in the records described in 24.2-6.

9

$\mathcal{T}$enants and Crofters

9.1 The chances are that your ancestors were tenants rather than owners of where they stayed. Since 1855, the Valuation Rolls, described in 8.43-46, record most, though not all, tenants in Scotland and you will look for your more recent ancestors in that record. Unfortunately, prior to 1855, no consistent record was kept of tenancies. Also, records that were kept and that have survived are largely of tenancies of farms. Records of ownership of property, described in 8.1-42, often contain incidental references to tenancies, sometimes identifying a piece of land by the name of its tenant. Between 1832 and 1918, registers of voters state if the voter was a tenant and of what property (see 24.2-6). This chapter will deal with other records which you might examine if your ancestor was a tenant, especially a tenant-farmer. Remember that many people, such as farm workers, would be neither tenant nor owner of where they stayed.

Rentals and Tacks

9.2 A tenancy was usually constituted by a document known as a tack, but there was no register of tacks, and, after a tenancy had run its course, no legal necessity to preserve the tack. However, some have survived in private papers, as have rentals, in which many landlords, particularly big landowners, listed their tenanted properties. Rentals, like the older valuation rolls, may sometimes just name the lands and not the occupiers, and, though they generally name tenants, these will only be the heads of household and will commonly omit any designation.

9.3 Rentals and tacks are records of private individuals. You need to know which family owned the property of which your ancestor may have been a tenant, and then to find out if the records of that family have survived. This leads us again to the GDs, described in 4.18-19. In most of the longer GDs, there will be a separate section for estate papers, which should include any records of tenancies. The Breadalbane Muniments (GD.112) have a particularly good series of rentals and tacks for north Perthshire and part of Argyll dating from the 16th century. You should also consult the Clio textbase under 'rental(s)'.

9.4 If the GDs fail you, you might wish to check for rentals in certain public records.

9.5 The records of the Commissioners of Crown Estates (CR) include records of two estates which belonged to the Duke of Gordon - Glenlivet and Fochabers. Look in the CR repertory under CR.6 and CR.8. There are rentals between 1770 and 1890. As the Duke of Gordon's own muniments are also in the SRO (GD.44), you have a fair chance of finding a reference to an ancestor who was a Gordon tenant.

9.6 Estates forfeited because of their owners' support for the Jacobite cause in 1745 were administered by the Barons of Exchequer and records of that administration are preserved in the Exchequer records. To see if these estates include one relevant to your research, look in the inventory of the Forfeited Estates papers (E.700-788) at the contents list under 'Particular Management' or the location list under county and parish. There are rentals of all the estates (with contents lists by name of the forfeited owners) for the period 1747-76 under the reference E.707 and rentals of particular estates under the reference number for that estate. These rentals include some 'judicial rentals' which are records of statements by tenants about their tenancies and which supply slightly more information than an ordinary rental. There is also a published list of tenants of farms on some of these estates in 1755 in *Statistics of the Annexed Estates* (copies may be purchased from the SRO).

9.7 There are also some rentals in the RH series. Look in the repertory for RH.9/3 which lists most of these miscellaneous rentals and for RH.11 which lists a few rentals among local court records.

9.8 Rentals provide an example of how similar records can be found in a variety of record groups. For instance, say your ancestors were tenants on the estate of Callendar near Falkirk in the 18th-century. You will find rentals dated 1717 in the RH series (RH.11/10/1), dated 1748 in the Forfeited Estates papers (E.761/1/3), and dated 1785-91 in the Forbes of Callendar muniments (GD.171/2100), now transmitted to The History Research Centre, Callendar House, Falkirk.

9.9 Estate records often include plans of the estate, on which the names of tenants might be annotated on their piece of land. Such plans in the SRO are in the Register House Plans series (RHP), described in 20.3. Look in the RHP card index in West Register House under the heading of the parish in which the relevant estate, farm or other property lay.

9.10 Tenants at the end of the 18th century may be found in the tax records discussed in 13.5-9, including a useful record of tenant-farmers in the record of taxes on work-horses (E.326/10).

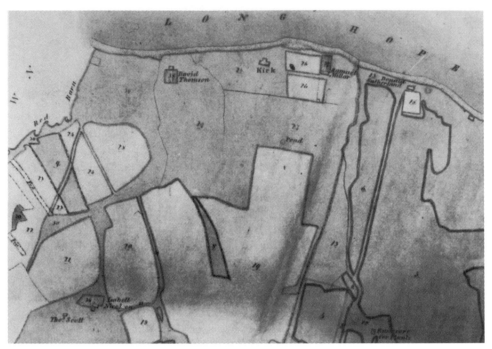

Part of plan of lands in South Walls, Orkney, showing names of tenants, 1823.
(RHP.2910)

Tenants in Trouble

9.11 Records of some tenants have survived because they failed to pay their rent or refused to leave at the end of their tenancy when the landlord wished to re-acquire the property. The landlord might then pursue the tenant in a court of law. Until 1747, this would be most likely a local court (see 11.49-51) which might well be the landlord's own court. After 1747, the court would be a sheriff or burgh court (see 11.36-40 and 11.48). The records of such cases are generally intermingled with those of other court cases, are not indexed and therefore may require a lot of searching. Separate records of such cases in the sheriff courts exist only from the later 19th century, when information about tenancies is more easily obtained from the Valuation Rolls. However, you may wish to investigate these records.

9.12 Look in the contents list of the repertory of the relevant sheriff court for 'Register of Sequestrations for Rent'. If there is no such entry, look up 'Register of Sequestrations', as that may include sequestrations for rent. These records most commonly start in 1867, but some start later, while Cupar (SC.20/11) starts in 1839. As a separate entity, records of cases of removal of tenants only occur in the 20th century - look for 'Summary Removing Court Books' in the repertory - except for the Dundee court where they start in 1885 (SC.45/30).

Crofters

9.13 Crofters are a class of agricultural tenant, for the most part in the Highlands and Islands. Records about crofters postdate the Valuation Rolls, but may provide a record of low-rent tenants omitted from the Valuation Rolls.

9.14 The records of the Royal Commission on the Highlands and Islands, 1883, are an important source of information about crofters. Look up the repertory of the Department of Agriculture and Fisheries (AF) and at AF.50 therein. There are two sets of relevant returns, AF.50/7 and AF.50/8. AF.50/7 consists of returns, bound by counties, of crofters. Within the county volume, the arrangement is alphabetical by estate. The information given includes the name of the township and/or croft, the name of each tenant, the number of families on the croft and the number of persons habitually residing in the croft. AF.50/8 consists of unbound returns of cottars, who are tenants of cottages without land attached. These returns are by estate, and, as well as giving the name of each cottar, specify their occupation or means of subsistence, eg 'supported by a son at sea – a Sailor' (AF.50/8/2).

Land Court

9.15 If your ancestor was a crofter after 1886 or a small agricultural tenant anywhere in Scotland after 1912, you might want to look at the records of the Scottish Land Court (LC) which has jurisdiction in certain matters relating to these landholdings. First read the introduction to the LC repertory. Most of the Land Court records are arranged by county. The records of each county include landholders books and court rolls. Particularly before 1912, the cases are predominantly for valuation of fair rent. Both the landholders books and the court rolls are indexed by the name of the applicant, ie the tenant or crofter. This gives this record a searching advantage over the Valuation Rolls in respect of tenants who applied to the Land Court.

10

Other Legal Transactions

10.1 During his lifetime, your ancestor may have been engaged in a variety of legal transactions, which required documents which bear his name - bonds, contracts of sale, contracts of partnership, and so forth. While there was generally no public compulsion to preserve such records of private enterprise, many such documents have survived. Your problem is to find any which relate to your ancestor.

10.2 Fortunately, there was and is a type of record which was created for the purpose of preserving such legal documents (or 'deeds'), though only if the parties wished. In the 16th century, it became the practice for most courts of law to have a register of deeds, in which such documents were copied, either simply to ensure their preservation or to facilitate a legal action grounded on the deed. The original document was also often kept by the court. Up to 1809, any court had power to register deeds. After that date, only the Court of Session, sheriff courts and royal burgh courts had the power. If you are looking for a deed which you hope will have been copied into a register of deeds, you will need to look at both the register compiled in the Court of Session and the registers of any courts which had jurisdiction where your ancestor lived or was engaged in business. Any legal document might be copied into these registers. Deeds are arranged therein by date of registration, not the date of the deed. Some deeds have been registered years after the date of the deed. Thus, in seeking a deed which you hope has been registered, you may have to search several records and a longish date period, often without the aid of indexes.

Books of Council and Session

10.3 The register attached to the Court of Session is known both as the 'Books of Council and Session' and, simply, 'The Register of Deeds' (RD). Indexing of this huge Register is patchy. We will consider its accessibility before and after 1660.

The Register of Deeds before 1660

10.4 While the Register of Deeds is officially regarded as starting in 1554, it was not a tidy start. Deeds had been previously registered in other Court of Session court books and some continued to be so. There are calendars available of deeds in the Acta Dominorum Concilii 1501-1514 (CS.5), Acta Dominorum Concilii et Sessionis 1532-1559 (CS.6) and Acts and Decreets 1542-1581 (indexed, CS.7). Order by the CS reference and volume number.

10.5 There is a Calendar of Deeds in the Register of Deeds itself for the period between 1554 and 1595, in a series of volumes with a lot of date overlap . These are partly indexed in separate volumes. Order the Register volume containing the deed by RD.1 and the volume number.

10.6 Between 1596 and 1660, there are no calendars or indexes, and thus, to search the Register of Deeds, you will have to use its minute books. Before 1660, there are five series of minute books, partly concurrent. Look up the Register of Deeds repertory under the reference RD.6. Each of the five series appears under a name: 'Scott', 'Gibson', 'Hay', 'Dounie', and 'Brown', the names of the offices which compiled the Register. Order out the minute books which cover the date period you are searching. Each minute book is arranged by date of registration and gives that date, an abbreviation of the type of document, and the surnames only of the principal parties, expressed as if parties in a legal dispute. If you find a promising entry, order out the RD.1 volume which covers the date and which, according to the repertory, bears the same office name as the minute book. For example, when you are looking for an ancestor named Kincaid, you find in a Hay minute book under the date 'undecimo decemb: 1639' (undecimo being Latin for eleven) an entry 'Gray qr Kincaid - disch' ('qr' is short for 'contra'). Therefore you order out RD.1/524, which, the repertory tells you, is the Hay volume covering November 1639 to July 1640. In this volume, the dates of registration are placed prominently and the names of the parties are placed in the margins, and therefore the entry is easy to find. The deed is a discharge by Jean Kincaid, relict of umquhile Mr Thomas Gray, advocate, of payment in terms of their marriage contract.

The Register of Deeds from 1661

10.7 From 1661 to 1811, the Register of Deeds was compiled in three separate but concurrent series, known as 'DAL', 'DUR', and 'MACK', which are abbreviated forms of the names of the three offices which compiled the Register. As there is no content distinction between the three offices, any deed might be registered by any of them and you have to search all three. Fortunately, the indexes are to all three series in one.

10.8 From 1661-1696, there are printed annual indexes published this century. Copies may be obtainable through your local library and may be purchased from the SRO. Indexes have also been prepared for the years 1697-1702, 1705-7 and 1714, but are available for sale only on microfiche. The style of these indexes varies, but all provide the name and designation of each party, and the volume and folio number of the deed. All principal parties are indexed. To order out a volume of the Register, if the volume number in the index is preceded by DAL, order by RD.2 and the volume number; if DUR, order by RD.3 and the volume number; if MACK, order by RD.4 and the volume number. Occasionally, a deed has been omitted from the volume of the Register but has survived among the original documents kept as 'warrants' of the Register. If the index says 'warrant' instead of a volume number, order by RD.12 (for DAL), RD.13 (for DUR), or RD.14 (for MACK), a number for the year (1 for 1661, 2 for 1662 and so on up to 151 for 1811), and the warrant number, eg RD.13/33/no. 547. For warrants after 1811, you order by RD.15, the year number which is 1 for 1812, 2 for 1813 and so on, and the warrant number, if you know it. If you want to order an original deed, but do not know its warrant number, you can order by the RD number, the year number (as before), the month and day of registration, and the names of the parties.

10.9   A regular series of indexes commences again in 1770. Prior to that there are modern indexes for 1750-2 and a manuscript index for 1765. Thus, most of the 18th-century Register of Deeds is unindexed.

10.10   To search for a deed registered in the unindexed years, you have again to use minute books, of which there are three concurrent series to search: DAL (RD.7/1), DUR (RD.7/2) and MACK (RD.7/3). Look at the repertory for the reference numbers of minute books covering specific dates. Again, you have to browse through the minute books, all three sets, each arranged chronologically by date of registration, to find an entry which may seem to be relevant. The later minute books state the Christian names as well as surnames of parties, which helps. To exemplify: you will find in a DAL minute book (RD.7/1/5) on 30 March 1714, an entry 'Con^t of Mar Arnot & Spalden', which leads you to the volume of the Register referenced RD.2/103/2, in which you will find the date of registration at the top of each page and the names of parties at the head of each deed; and thus you find the contract of marriage, dated in 1694, between Archibald Arnott, chirurgeon apothecary in Dundee, and Catherine Spalding, daughter of Mr John Spalding, minister in Dundee. In a MACK minute book (RD.7/3/10) on 3 July 1750, you find 'Latter Will George Brodie to Katherine Brodie'. The will, which is in RD.4/176/2, does not appear to be in the Commissary Court records, and is the will of a soldier, signed at Breda in 1748, bequeathing his property to his four sisters.

10.11   Annual contemporary indexes have been compiled to the Register of Deeds since 1770. Their main disadvantage is that they index granters only. Alongside the name and brief designation of the granter, there is the name of the grantee, the sort of deed, dates of deed and registration and the volume and folio number. In the RD.2, 3 and 4 series, often one volume number is allocated to one calendar year, while the amount of deeds in that year requires two volumes, parts 1 and 2. Thus when, in the volume column of the index, you find (eg) an entry '2/240' with 'Dur' in an adjacent column, you order out RD.3/240/2. From 1812 on, you will be glad to hear, there are no longer the three separate offices, and the Register of Deeds exists in one series: order by RD.5 and the volume number. There is a set of these annual indexes up to 1850 in the Historical Search Room. You must go down to the Legal Search Room to search the indexes from 1851 and then return to the Historical Search Room to order out the requisite volume of the Register.

10.12 A common entry in the minute books is 'pro' for 'protest', a particular step in some actions for debt and often entered in registers of deeds. Protests are not included in the post-1770 indexes, and therefore to search for them, you will need to continue to use the minute books. From 1812, there is a separate Register of Protests (RD.17) which you search by means of its minute books (RD.18).

Sheriff Court Registers of Deeds

10.13 Extending your search for a deed to the registers of deeds kept by lesser courts may not be simple. There are a variety of courts and hardly any indexes. The next most important registers of deeds are those of the sheriff courts. Not all sheriff courts kept a register of deeds, but there is at least one for each sheriffdom. As usual, look first in the repertory of the records of a relevant sheriff court to see if it has a register of deeds. These registers of deeds vary tremendously in their earliest date and in how well they have survived. The earliest surviving is Perth (SC.49) which starts in 1570. The majority of sheriff courts have, as well as the registers of deeds themselves, minute books and warrants thereof, but not necessarily all three concurrently. For example, the Wigtown sheriff court (SC.19) has minute books from 1636, warrants from 1690, but no register until 1809. More commonly, minute books post-date their register and its warrants. From 1809, these registers were kept in a consistent form and such indexes as exist mainly date from then, but largely this record is unindexed. Check first to see if there is an index for your sheriff court and date or if a relevant volume of the register has an internal contents list or whether there is a contemporary minute book. Otherwise, you will have to sift through a register or box of original warrants of relevant date. The sheriff courts also have separate registers of protests from 1809 (some earlier), which are unindexed.

Burgh Registers of Deeds

10.14 The SRO holds registers of deeds for over half the royal burghs. Look in the B repertory at the contents list of the records of the burgh where your ancestor was to see if there is a register of deeds. The dates of these vary considerably, starting with Edinburgh in 1561 (B.22/8). They continue into the 20th century. Very few have minute books. If you are lucky, the appropriate volume may include an index or contents list. If not, look for the names of the parties in the margin beside or at the head of each entry in the register. A few burghs kept not only a register of deeds but also concurrently a register of probative writs, which was a class of deed. If so, that should also be consulted.

Commissary Courts Registers of Deeds

10.15 If you are searching for a deed before 1809, you might look at the Commissary Court registers of deeds. Between them, they cover the whole of Scotland, except that the Wigtown court has no register of deeds, while for Aberdeen and the Isles only warrants survive. Look at para 6.6 to find out which commissary court(s) served the county in which your ancestor lived. Then look at its (or their) contents list(s) in the CC repertory. Look carefully: there may be a separate register of probative writs; there may or may not be minute books. Many of these registers have gaps; if so, look also at the warrants of these registers. A few of the volumes may have contents lists. In terms of contents, there is no difference between these registers of deeds and those of other courts. You have to wade through many documents relating to debt to find the occasional marriage contract or will.

Local Courts Registers of Deeds

10.16 If you are looking for a deed dated earlier than 1748, then you might also look at the RH.11 repertory, to see if the records of a relevant 'local court' therein listed include a register of deeds. There is an index of courts by their place-name in the repertory. The lists of court records note not only registers of deeds, but also the existence of deeds in other court books. For example, the regality of Kilwinning has a register of deeds for 1620-51 and 1664-96, part of the gap being filled with deeds entered in a court book. There are no indexes, but contents lists are noted when they occur.

Deeds in Gifts and Deposits

10.17 Many deeds are scattered throughout the Gifts and Deposits and similar collections (see 4.18-19).

$\mathcal{L}$*itigants*

11.1 Compiling registers of deeds was only a subsidiary part of the work of a court and the records of the main business of courts of law may contain information valuable to the ancestor-hunter If your ancestor ran into debt or was of a disputatious nature and sufficiently prosperous, he probably got himself involved in litigation, and you will want to look for him in the records of those courts which dealt with legal disputes between private parties

11.2 Your initial problem is which court? There are courts which heard cases arising from any part of Scotland - the Court of Session, the Privy Council, the Admiralty Court, the Court of Exchequer. There were courts with a jurisdiction which was restricted to a particular administrative area - sheriff courts, commissary courts, burgh courts, Justice of the Peace courts, the 'franchise' courts. As most cases could be raised in more than one court and there were often appeals from a lower to a higher court, you may have to pursue your search in the records of several courts. It is difficult to give general advice on which court to start on. Maritime causes were heard by the Admiralty Court, cases involving marriage were heard by the Commissary Court of Edinburgh until 1830 (see 5.18-20), thereafter by the Court of Session; but apart from those, if the matter in dispute was minor, such as a small debt, you are best to start with a local court and, if the dispute was more significant, with the Court of Session

Court of Session

11.3 Let us start with the highest civil court in Scotland, the Court of Session. It has a vast bulk of records, which are desperately undersupplied with straightforward guides and are arranged in a complicated manner because that is the way the Court worked. Until 1821, the records of the Court were created within different offices, usually three concurrently. The cases were and are divided into two categories, those cases of which the final decree is 'extracted' and those of which it is not. If a decree was extracted, then it was copied into the Register of Acts and Decreets and the papers in the case preserved as 'extracted processes'. The records of all other cases, whether they reached decree or not, were preserved as 'unextracted processes'. There is no distinction in content between extracted and unextracted cases or between the various offices. Consequently, you may have to examine several sets of records, where you might expect one. To complicate matters further, at various times there have been divisions and separate departments of the Court of Session, with their own records. It is therefore difficult to explain simply how to gain access to the Court of Session records. However, we shall try, though you will still have to refer to the staff for further advice!

11.4 You had best start by looking at the modern class list of the Court of Session records, though it is incomplete and it may initially confuse you further. Alternatively or as well, look at the description of the Court of Session records in appendix 5 to the *Annual Report of the Keeper of the Records of Scotland, 1972*. Both summarise the records briefly, tell you the class numbers, and serve as an introduction. To find out the covering dates of the volumes of the Register of Acts and Decreets and minute books, you may have to consult one of the other guides such as a manuscript 'Repertory of Judicial Records' (kept in the Historical Search Room).

11.5 Your first task is to find out if there was a case before the Court of Session in which your ancestor was a party. Though there are some modern indexes, you will mostly have to look at the Court minute books and other imperfect guides. There are various problems. Often the cases will be described only by the surnames of the parties; indexes are usually of pursuers only, which is awkward if your ancestor was the defender; cases often change their names as they progress; cases often took several years to progress. Thus, Campbell v Macdonald, 1676, may later appear as Macdonald v Campbell, 1681. Though you may find short cuts, you will usually have to start by searching a minute book to ascertain if a case was heard by the Court, and persevere from there.

Court of Session before 1660

11.6 There are general minute books which note all the cases before the Court of Session, and particular minute books which note the cases dealt with by a particular office. Before 1650, the offices are called Scott, Gibson and Hay; between then and 1659, Brown and Durie. Because some of these minute books are damaged and therefore incomplete, you should check both general and particular ones. (If there is no surviving minute book, you can but read through the volumes of the Acts and Decreets.) The minute books are arranged chronologically and, under each date, list each legal action by the surnames of the opposing parties. The General Minute Books also supply the name of the relevant office, while the particular minute books will also tell you what happened to the action in the court on that day.

11.7 To illustrate, in a general minute book (cs.8/3) at 3 July 1579 there is an entry 'act betx Hammiltoun q^r Kynneir Gibson', which means that the Court that day heard an action between parties named Hamilton and Kinnear and that the case was recorded by Gibson's office. If you look in the Gibson particular minute book for that date (cs.10/1) you will find 'Hamilton q^r Kynneir – decernit' which confirms that there was a case between those parties on that date and that decree was granted. You then have to look in the Repertory of Judicial Records for the Gibson volume of the Register of Acts and Decreets (cs.7) which includes 3 July 1579 (cs.7/76). As you do not have a folio reference, you look in the volume for the date (which is expressed in Latin) and the name of the parties in the margin; and you find a decree in favour of John Hammiltoun of Drumry against a tenant David Kynneir to remove from the lands of Craigfudies; which may or may not be what you want.

Court of Session 1661-1912

11.8 To find a case, first go to the general minute books. Until 1781, these are in manuscript (CS.16). From 1782, they are printed (CS.17). The manuscript ones are not indexed and you have to wade through the entries until you find one that seems relevant. The printed ones, which are annual, are indexed. These indexes are to all parties, distinguishing pursuers by the letter 'p' and defenders by the letter 'd', but give the surname only, except for some common surnames. The Christian names, if given, may be in an abbreviated form, eg 'Ro' for 'Robert'. In the text of these minute books, there are further abbreviations for legal terms, such as 'P' for petition and 'D' for decree. The staff will advise you further on these.

Bangor, North Wales, master and owner of the schooner 'Agnes and Helen,' of Beaumaris, AG John Dobbie, contractor in Leith. Summons signed on 24th October last, *p* Baxter. A. & G. V. Mann, A.

INNER HOUSE.

FIRST DIVISION.

Wednesday, 31st October 1883.

B.

Act admitting Janet Young or Auld, residing at Bridgend, Kilwinning, to the benefit of the Poors Roll, to enable her to carry on an action of divorce against her husband, Robert C. Auld, sometime baker in Troon, and now or lately residing in the United States of America or elsewhere furth of Scotland, *p* R. K. Galloway. J. Pairman, A.

Intimation that a petition has been presented by (1), Elizabeth Steele or Ramsay, residing at Woodbank, Largs, relict of the deceased John Ramsay, writer in Alloa, with consent of Ebenezer Ramsay, residing at Woodbank, Largs, for his interest ; (2), Alexander Stewart, cotton VOL. CIII.

Session 21st J Steele, someti presently in E James Steele Hill Steele, p land, son of tl consent of his Guthrie Ramsa Steele and W Greenock, fro under the tru ment and co petition) exec Steele, shipbi the appointme the trust-estat disposition an *p* Pearson. J

SECO]

Wednesda

Act admitting 14 Tower Stre fit of the Po carry on a l M'Gilp, residin J. Pairman, A.

Excerpt from Court of Session minute book. (CS.17/1/103)

11.9 In both manuscript and printed minute books, the entries are detailed and will therefore tell you if the case is one that will interest you or not. In the margin (manuscript) or as a heading (printed) there are some initials, eg 'H.J.L.', which are the clerk's mark, which you may need to trace the case further. Then there are some details about the case, the names and designations of the parties, and finally the names of the procurator (advocate) and judge. If you want more detail, you will then look elsewhere for the record of the case, which will usually be described by the pursuer's surname v the defender's surname.

11.10 First try the indexes to the Unextracted Processes. There are four card indexes divided chronologically, so look in the one that covers the date of the case (or two if the date is near the borderline). The first three of these are arranged by surname and chronologically within surname, while the fourth is arranged by surname and christian name. These cards give an old reference, eg 2P.Y.5/3, which you will have to convert into the present call number. The first number and letter will always convert into a CS number, eg 2P becomes CS.247. The rest of the old reference may still be used or may have to be converted into a running number: the staff will advise.

11.11 If you cannot find your case in these card indexes, next try what is called the Carmichael and Elliot arrangement of processes. Again there is a card index, arranged by surnames only (in various original spellings) and with an old reference which has to be converted to a present-day one.

11.12 Still no success? You now want to try the Register of Acts and Decreets. How to search this depends on the date you are searching.

11.13 *Up to 1810* look again at the clerk's mark which you found in the minute book. Refer to a guide to clerks' marks which will tell you whether this particular clerk was employed in the DAL, DUR or MACK offices. You now want to look at the relevant extractor's minute book. Of these, DAL is now CS.19; DUR is CS.23; and MACK is CS.27. An entry gives simply the date and surnames of the parties. If you find a relevant entry, order out the equivalent volume of the Register of Acts and Decreets, which was kept in the three offices, the familiar DAL (CS.18), DUR (CS.22), and MACK (CS.26). If you want to see the warrants or papers in the case (known as 'extracted processes'), you order by CS.21 (DAL), CS.25 (DUR) or CS.29 (MACK) plus the date and the names of the parties. These processes may not add anything to what you find in the Register, in which written pleadings are given at great length. A 17th-century judge described the bulk of decreets as 'nauseous'!

11.14 *Since 1810* there are annual indexes to the Register of Acts and Decreets. Within each year and within each initial letter of surname, the order is chronological. The entry tells you the type of case, the names (usually just surnames) of the parties and the date the decree was extracted. You then have to find the relevant CS number and the volume number of that CS series which includes that date. The equivalent extracted process is ordered out by the relevant CS number, date and names of parties. These processes may include information not in the Register.

11.15 Let us now look at some examples.

11.16 In a General Minute Book (CS.16/1/54) under the date 11th February 1721 you find an entry 'Decreet in absence Elizabeth and Helen Monteiths Daughters to umqull Alexander Monteith of Todshaugh chirurgeon in Edinburgh and their husbands contra John Fultoun chirurgeon in Douglas'. You do not find this case in the Unextracted Processes or Carmichael and Elliot indexes, but in the DAL Extractors Minute Book for that date (CS.19/1/3) you find 'D[= decree] Monteiths q Fulton'. Therefore you order out the volume of the Register of Acts and Decreets, series DAL, for that date (CS.18/204) and look through it to find the full report of the case, which supplies the names of the ladies' husbands and shows that the case was brought to retrieve debts owed to the deceased Alexander Monteith for 'drugs and medicaments furnished by him'. You may also order out the extracted process relevant to the case, which is CS.21/1721 February 11/Monteiths v Fulton.

11.17 In a General Minute Book (CS.16/1/132) under the date 27th January 1768 you find a case brought by Christian Allan, daughter to James Allan, late bailie of Hamilton, against John McNeill, schoolmaster in Hamilton. You look up the Unextracted Process card index and find 'Allan, Christian v McNiel 1767 Adams Mack A.1/101'. This number converts into CS.229/A.1/101 which you order out and find that the action was for non-payment of rent of a house owned by the pursuer in the Castlewynd of Hamilton. (You may then try the Register of Sasines in the hope of finding more information.)

11.18 Having looked up the name 'Lindsay' in the index to the 1815-16 printed general minute book (CS.17/1/35) you find a case heard by the First Division of the Court on 28 February 1816 'D[ecree] in ab[sence] David Freer, W.S. AG[ainst] Sam[uel] Lindsay, brewer in Dunkeld'. The clerk's mark is M.H.B. You then look in the Acts and Decreets index for 1816 and find the entry 'Freer v Lindsay' with the date of extract 16 July 1816. 'M.H.B.' is the mark for volumes of the Register of Acts and Decreets referenced CS.39 and extracted processes referenced CS.40. You order out CS.39/22 and look through this volume until you find the decree. The case is a simple one of debt.

11.19 Divorce cases were the responsibility of the Court of Session after 1830 and to find them up to 1912 you look initially at the printed minute books. You are looking for the divorce case of a couple named McKay. The index in the minute book for 1884 (CS.17/1/103) leads you to an entry under the date 22nd January 1884, describing a decree of divorce in favour of Janet Rankin, or Lean, or Mckay, residing in Creetown, against James McKay, residing at Xenia, in the State of Ohio, in the United States of America. The minute also names their daughter, and his sister and mother, who live in Newton Stewart. As you want more information, you look up the index to Unextracted Processes and find a card 'McKay, Janet Rankin or Lean or, v Mckay, Divorce 1882, 2P.Mc.14/2' which number converts into CS.247/4184. You order out this process and discover that the defender went to America to gain employment but has not been heard of for several years.

Court of Session since 1912

11.20 After 1912, there are annual indexes to the Unextracted Processes in book
form, and you may prefer to go straight to this index and then to the index to
the Acts and Decreets, though the General Minute Books are still the best
guide to which cases were heard by the Court of Session. Note that the
indexes to Acts and Decreets after 1900 are only available in the Legal Search
Room. The annual indexes to the Unextracted Processes are, as usual, indexes
to pursuers only, giving also the nature of the process, the name of the
defender and the year the case was called, which will be earlier than the year
of the index.

Bill Chamber

11.21 You may have come across cases in the minute books which you have not
been able to trace or you simply wish to search further among the Court of
Session records. There are some guides which we have not yet consulted. Most
notably there are indexes to the Bill Chamber processes (CS.271), the Bill
Chamber being a court within the Court of Session. The CS class-list explains
its functions. There are two indexes (of pursuers) overlapping, the one
covering the dates 1670-1852, the other 1684-1848. In one you find an entry
'Balderston, Jean, or Wise & ors [others] v Thomas Leishman, 1773, 8,170', this
number being that of the process. You order out CS.271/8170 and find that the
case is an appeal by Jean and her sisters, who are named, along with their
husbands, against a decree in favour of Leishman by the barony court of
Falkirk.

Jury Court

11.22 The Jury Court existed between 1815 and 1850 to hear cases referred to a jury
by the Court of Session. There is a guide to its processes in a list thereof in
roughly alphabetical order. You will find entries such as '36 Anderson, George
v James McHaffie 1834', which process is ordered out by the reference
CS.311/36, and is found to be an action for defamation.

Accountant of Court

11.23 The office of Accountant of Court (records from 1739) has responsibility in
regard to the supervision of estates of children and other persons unable to
administer their own affairs. If you are seeking actions concerning the
guardianship of infants or the appointment of factors loco tutoris, you should
examine these records (CS.313-317). You will remember that a tutor is
appointed to administer the affairs of a fatherless child (see 7.5-21). If you fail
to find a record of the appointment of a tutor in the record of Retours, you
should try the records of the Accountant of Court. There are indexes (see the
CS repertory). You may find sufficient detail in the printed minute book,
however.

Sequestrations

11.24 Over the years, a sadly large number of Scotsmen have become bankrupt and methods have had to be found to satisfy their creditors. The earlier main legal method, cessio bonorum, was largely superseded by sequestration which dates from 1771. Since then, there have been regular reforms, attempting to provide justice for all parties concerned. These regular changes in the system mean that there is a variety of paths to follow to find a particular sequestration case. In some cases, the bankrupt will be the pursuer; in some cases, a creditor.

Bankrupts prior to 1839

11.25 Prior to 1839, to look for a bankruptcy case among the Court of Session records, you can use the procedures described above for all cases. From August 1783, you have the alternative of looking first in the printed index to the General Register of Inhibitions (see 11.56-58), as from that date all petitions for sequestration had to be recorded in that register. It is the bankrupt who is indexed and therefore you will find out if it is worth searching the Court of Session records for the case. An additional path is to look at the published and indexed *List of Court of Session Productions* (List and Index Society), which lists business books (CS.96) found in Court of Session processes. These books include sederunt books compiled by the trustees in bankruptcy and the entries in the *List* provide the reference of the sequestration process to which the sederunt book refers.

Bankrupts 1839-1913

11.26 For this period, an alphabetical list of sequestrated bankrupts has been compiled from various sources by Glasgow University Archives. First, look at this list (there is a copy in the Search Room) to see if your ancestor is in it. If his name is not there, there is no point in going further. This list provides the bankrupt's name, trade, place and date of sequestration; and, for some bankrupts, a code number, which you should note if it begins with the letter 'A'. Your next step is to read 'A Guide to Scottish Sequestrations, 1839-1913' which is available in the Search Room. This provides detailed advice on how to search for a sequestration case. If your bankrupt has the 'A' code number mentioned above, use the second of the two flow charts in that guide.

11.27 Sheriff courts also dealt with bankruptcy cases. Look at the contents list of the records of the relevant sheriff court (SC) for 'Register of Sequestrations'. There is a useful guide to these in the Court of Session records, as after 1840 sheriff clerks made returns to the Court of Session of sequestrations depending before their court (CS.283, 331 and 332).

Privy Council

11.28 The Court of Session was, in origin, an offshoot of the Privy Council, which had judicial as well as administrative functions. The Privy Council continued to act in a judicial capacity up to 1707, issuing decrees, or making an effort 'to agree the parties', or referring a case to the Court of Session or a lower court. It tended to be the better-off complainant who took a case to the Privy Council.

11.29   *The Register of the Privy Council of Scotland* is published up to 1691, each volume being fully indexed. If you are looking for a case between 1545 and 1691, look up the name of the party in the index of the printed volume for the relevant period. The printed text is quite full, but if you want to see the original, order by PC.1, up to August 1610, or PC.2, after that date, and the volume number given in the PC repertory for the date of that entry.

11.30   Between 1692 and 1695, you have no choice but to look in the original volumes of the Registers of Decreta (PC.2/24-26): look for the brief description of each entry in the margin. Between 1696 and 1707, look in the minute books (PC.4/2-3) which describe all the business of the Council, not just the judicial business. There you will find such entries as 'Lybell Bruce of Pitterthie agt Corstorphine of Neydie Called and remitted to the Judge ordinar' (26 January 1697), which will show if it is worthwhile examining the PC.2 volumes.

Admiralty Court

11.31   The Admiralty Court had jurisdiction in all maritime and seafaring cases, both civil and criminal, until 1830, when its civil jurisdiction was transferred to the Court of Session. If your ancestor was a shipowner or shipmaster or merchant who traded overseas, then he may have been involved in an action before the Admiralty Court.

11.32   Look at the Admiralty Court repertory (AC). The records which concern you are the decreets and processes (AC.7, 8, 9, 10, 15), to which there are guides in the form of roughly chronological lists of cases.

11.33   AC.7 consists of volumes of decreets, 1627-1830. To obtain the guide to them, order out AC.7/107, which lists the surnames of pursuer and defender, the date and the volume number; eg 'Mitchell. Mackenzie. 2 July 1725. Vol 30'. To see that decreet, you order out AC.7/30. If you are lucky, the volume will have a contents list, giving the folio number on which the decreet starts.

11.34   AC.8, 9, 10 and 15, which date from or after 1702, each have a modern contents list available in the Search Room. These give the decree or process number, the names of the pursuer and defender and the year; eg 'AC.10 563 Brymer, Magnus v James Hutton 1779'. This is a case brought by an apprentice sailmaker in Leith who joined the navy and was then incarcerated at the instance of his master until he found someone to guarantee the completion of his apprenticeship. The majority of cases are less interesting, being mainly for payment.

Court of Exchequer

11.35 Between 1708 and 1856 (when its jurisdiction was transferred to the Court of Session), the Court of Exchequer dealt with revenue cases, including debts to the Crown, seizure of smuggled goods and prosecutions for illicit brewing and distilling. Unfortunately, its records generally provide little information about individuals and there are no indexes. To investigate, look first at the minute books (E.351) which will tell the names but not the designations of the parties in the cases. If you find a case which seems relevant, look further at the books of orders (E.352), the enrolled or original informations, which may provide designations but which are in various rather abstruse series (see the repertory – E.358-368), and the affidavits, which can be informative but many have not survived (E.376). If your ancestor owed money to the Crown between 1711 and 1827, there may be an inventory of his property in a series referenced E.371.

Sheriff Courts

11.36 Apart from the Court of Session, the court in which your ancestor would most likely be a litigant would be a sheriff court. There are the following sheriff courts, each with jurisdiction over all or part of a county. Each has its own repertory.

County	Sheriff Courts
Aberdeen	Aberdeen (SC.1); Peterhead (SC.4)
Angus (Forfar)	Arbroath (SC.43); Dundee (SC.45); Forfar (SC.47)
Argyll	Campbeltown (SC.50); Dunoon (SC.51); Fort William (SC.52); Inveraray (SC.54); Oban (SC.57); Tobermory (SC.59)
Ayr	Ayr (SC.6); Kilmarnock (SC.7)
Banff	Banff (SC.2)
Berwick	Duns (SC.60)
Bute	Rothesay (SC.8)
Caithness	Wick (SC.14)
Clackmannan	Alloa (SC.64)
Dumfries	Dumfries (SC.15)
Dunbarton	Dumbarton (SC.65)
East Lothian (Haddington)	Haddington (SC.40)
Edinburgh City	Edinburgh (SC.39); Leith (SC.69)
Fife	Cupar (SC.20); Dunfermline (SC.21); Kirkcaldy (SC.23)
Glasgow	Glasgow (SC.36)
Inverness	Fort William (SC.28); Inverness (SC.29); Lochmaddy (SC.30); Portree (SC.32)
Kincardine	Stonehaven (SC.5)

County	Sheriff Courts
Kinross	Kinross (SC.22)
Kirkcudbright	Kirkcudbright (SC.16); Dumfries (SC.17)
Lanark	Airdrie (SC.35); Glasgow (SC.36); Hamilton (SC.37); Lanark (SC.38)
Midlothian (Edinburgh)	Edinburgh (SC.39)
Moray (Elgin)	Elgin (SC.26)
Nairn	Nairn (SC.31)
Orkney	Kirkwall (SC.11 - in Kirkwall); Orkney and Shetland (SC.10 - 17th century only)
Peebles	Peebles (SC.42)
Perth	Dunblane (SC.44); Perth (SC.49)
Renfrew	Greenock (SC.53); Paisley (SC.58)
Ross and Cromarty	Cromarty (SC.24); Dingwall (SC.25); Stornoway (SC.33); Tain (SC.34)
Roxburgh	Jedburgh (SC.62)
Selkirk	Selkirk (SC.63)
Shetland	Lerwick (SC.12 - in Lerwick); Orkney and Shetland (SC.10 - 17th century only)
Stirling	Falkirk (SC.66); Stirling (SC.67)
Sutherland	Dornoch (SC.9)
West Lothian (Linlithgow)	Linlithgow (SC.41)
Wigtown	Stranraer (SC.L8); Wigtown (SC.19)

11.37 First, decide which sheriff court(s) had jurisdiction where your ancestor was, and then look at the relevant sheriff court repertory. In its contents list, look at the records of the 'Ordinary Court', which are usually at the start of the repertory.

11.38 There is little consistency among the various sheriff courts in the names they gave their series of records or in the contents thereof. Even within one series, there may be considerable variety in the sort of detail provided. There is tremendous variation in the commencement date of surviving records and there may be unexplained gaps. The only modern indexes to sheriff court cases are to Midlothian decrees (SC.39/8) 1830-1900 and to Perthshire processes (SC.44/22) 1809-1900; though some volumes have contents lists.

11.39 Depending on what categories of records have been created by each sheriff court and on what has survived, to search for a case you may have to look at minute books, act books, diet books or court books, around the appropriate date, or, from the late 19th century, registers of ordinary actions and of summary applications. It will be up to you to decide how to proceed. There will often also be a register of decrees and one or more series of processes.

11.40 For instance, if you are looking for a case in the Sheriff Court of Hamilton after 1770, you should look first at the minute books (SC.37/4) to find the case, then at the act books (SC.37/2) for details of the case, and, if the case reached decree, at the decree books (SC.37/7) for more detail. You may also want to search for the process (SC.37/8).

11.41 The sort of cases you may be seeking in the sheriff court records are actions for aliment, affiliation orders, registration of irregular marriages, small debt, workmen's compensation. Sometimes these cases will be found mixed among all the other cases, sometimes they will be in a separate volume or series. For example, the Aberdeen sheriff court has a separate alimentary register 1903-24 (SC.1/7/19) in the midst of the records of decrees.

11.42 Actions for registration of irregular marriages date after 1859 and are unlikely to provide information additional to that to be found in the official registers of marriages.

11.43 In a sheriff court repertory, the records of workmen's compensation cases, that is for compensation for personal injury by accident in course of employment, are usually placed separately from those of the ordinary court. They date from 1898.

Commissary Courts

11.44 As well as dealing with executry matters, the commissary courts had a civil jurisdiction until 1823. Most of the actions heard by the courts other than the Edinburgh Commissary Court (5.18-20) were for debt.

11.45 Look at the table at 6.6 which shows which commissary court had jurisdiction within which modern counties. Then look in the CC repertory for the list of records of the relevant commissariot. The records of civil actions are called act or diet books, minute books and registers of decrees, and processes. There are no indexes. All the cases should be noted in the Act or Diet Books, but often the record is brief and will probably not say what the action was about. The Registers of Decrees give a full report of the cases, but not all the cases reached decrees.

Justice of Peace Courts

11.46 A civil case could be brought before the Justices of Peace of the relevant county, but, apart from small debt cases (since 1795), the records of this civil jurisdiction are rather sparse, which is a pity as the JP courts sometimes heard cases of aliment.

11.47 If you want to search this record, look at the contents list of the JP repertory for the relevant county or city and then at the court books in the records of that JP court. The records of some of these courts have been transferred to local archives.

Burgh Courts

11.48 If your ancestor resided in a royal burgh, he might have been a litigant in the burgh court. Look at the list of records of the particular burgh in the B repertory, to see if these include court books or a register of decreets. The SRO does not hold such records for the majority of burghs, but they may be held by a local archive. These court books can vary tremendously in content, from simply stating the name of the parties to full copies of the decreets. The vast majority of the cases heard in the burgh courts were for debt. There are no indexes.

Franchise Courts

11.49 The Crown used to franchise local justice to certain landowners, who could hold courts in their own lands and administer justice over their vassals and tenants. There were four types of these courts - regality, barony, stewartry and bailiary. Most were abolished in 1747 and the rest thereafter quickly declined into insignificance.

11.50 Look at the RH.11 repertory. This has an index of courts, which directs you to the local court records in the RH.11 series and also those in other classes of records. If you find a required place-name in the index and then go to the list of records of that local court, the records of litigation you require will be usually described as 'court books' or 'minutes of court'. The reports of cases in these are generally rather summary, sometimes just giving the names of the parties, but you may be lucky. The commonest actions before such courts are for payment and between landlord and tenant.

11.51 These court books are not indexed and are compiled in a variety of handwritings which make them particularly difficult to decipher. However, a few of them have been published, such as those of the regality of Melrose (Scottish History Society).

Diligence

11.52 Your ancestor's name may also appear in the records of the procedures whereby the courts tried to enforce their decrees. For this purpose, a document registered for execution in a register of deeds (see 10.2) counts as a decree. The generic term for these procedures is diligence. The individual documents are known as 'letters of' that particular form of diligence. The commonest are letters of horning. You may be seeking such letters because you have come across a reference to them in a document or case record, or because you suspect that they may have followed on a registered deed or court decision, or just in a general trawl for your ancestors. They largely relate to debt situations.

11.53 Of the various forms of diligence, there are three main forms of which registers were kept and therefore provide consistent records in a consultative form.

These are registers of hornings, inhibitions and apprisings or adjudications. There were general registers for each, covering the whole of Scotland, and particular registers of hornings and inhibitions kept within counties and regalities. After 1781, there are indexes to the registers of inhibitions and adjudications. Otherwise, you have to search the minute books or, if there are no minute books, the record itself. Look at the Diligence (DI) repertory to see what volumes and minute books are available.

Hornings

11.54 Letters of horning charged a debtor to pay or perform as the court instructed. They were much used and affected most classes of society. If the debtor failed to obey the letters of horning, they could be registered, opening the way for sterner measures, including imprisonment and forfeiture of goods. Registration might be either in the general register of hornings or the particular register for the county or (until 1748) regality where the parties were. As there are no indexes, you have to know the approximate date and place for your search.

11.55 However, the minute books are clear and informative about the parties, who are expressed in the creditor against the debtor format, eg in the general minute book on 1st of April 1701 (expressed in Latin) we find an entry 'Mary Haigs Eldest Laull daughter of James Haigs Gairdner at Dalkeith Agt John Mair Portioner of Pinky commonly called Greinwalls' (DI.2/17). This turns out to be an untypical case, because when we get out the volume of the register for that date (DI.1/345) we find that Mair is being sued for a penalty for not fulfilling a contract to marry Mary Haigs.

Inhibitions

11.56 Inhibitions were designed (a) to prevent a debtor from disposing of his heritable property to the detriment of his creditor; and (b) to stop a husband's liability for his wife's debts. From 1783, petitions for sequestration were also recorded in the general register of inhibitions. Thus, this record is only worth investigating if your ancestor was likely to have owned land or a house, or had a broken marriage, or went bankrupt. The property is not named. Again you may have to investigate three registers – the general register of inhibitions, and the particular registers for the county (until 1869) or regality (until 1748). After 1869, there is only the general register. To search these up to 1780, you have to use the minute books, which are clear and detailed. From 1781, there are indexes, separate ones for the general register (printed up to 1868, then manuscript) and for the particular registers for each county (printed).

11.57 These are indexes of the parties inhibited or sequestrated, ie the debtor or the wife or the bankrupt. The indexes give the name and designation of the person inhibited or sequestrated, the name of the inhibiter (plus designation if a husband), the date, the volume number (in roman numerals) and the folio number (in arabic numerals). Within each surname, companies are indexed before individuals. Women are indexed by their maiden name. Sequestrations are distinguished by the abbreviation '*Seq.*' instead of '*Inhib.*'.

11.58 You order out by the DI series number, which you obtain from the repertory, and the volume number (converted into arabic). For example, in the index to the general register of inhibitions, you find DICKIE, John, merchant, Dunfermline. *Seq.* Mar. 19. 1788. -cciv.931' and therefore you order out DI.8/204 and look up folio 931: or in the index to the particular register for Haddington you find 'BEGBIE, Marion; *Inhib.* by James Telfer, Labourer, Haddington, her husband, Jan. 30. 1811-xxii.422.' and order out DI.60/22 and look up folio 422.

Apprisings and Adjudications

11.59 If a creditor wished to attach and obtain ownership of the heritable property of a debtor in satisfaction for a debt, then he had to obtain a decree of apprising (until 1672) or adjudication (from 1672) against the debtor. From 1636, these decrees were copied into a register (DI.13 and 14), the adjudications in a sensibly abbreviated form. Although these were decrees of the Court of Session, it is easier to trace apprisings and adjudications in these registers than in the records of the Court.

11.60 Until 1780, they have to be searched by means of the minute books, which are mostly nicely detailed, with the surname of the main debtor is the margin. The volume number and call number is found in the DI repertory. From 1781, there are indexes, printed up to 1868, thereafter manuscript. These index the debtor, supplying the names and designations of both debtor and creditor, the date, and volume and folio numbers: eg 'WEIR, Andrew, late candlemaker, Edinburgh, now abroad, and Janet Kettle, his spouse; *By* Janet Swanston, in East Register Street, Edinburgh, Apr.23.1818. -clxvi.74.' The repertory provides the reference DI.14/166. The adjudication starting on folio 74 therein does not, alas, tell us why Andrew is abroad, but does give a detailed description of the lodging house adjudged from the Weirs.

11.61 These decrees and their abbreviates specify the lands to be apprised or adjudged. Obviously, you will only want to inspect this register if your ancestor owned heritable property. It is quite useful to genealogists because of the practice of pursuing the heirs of deceased debtors. In these cases, the relationship of the heir or heirs to the deceased debtor will be explained. For example, in the minute book for 21st August 1754 (DI.15/15), you will find an entry labelled 'Macquaintances', which lists three members of that uncommon family who are pursued as heirs of an uncle and cousin named Forbes. The register (DI.14/97) supplies no further genealogical information to that which is in the minute book.

Imprisonment

11.62 Until 1880, it was quite common for debtors, who could not pay, to be imprisoned at the instance of their creditors. Thus, their names may appear in prison registers along with people accused of and found guilty of crimes (see 12.20-24).

Sanctuary

11.63 Until 1880, civil debtors might avoid diligence by taking sanctuary in the palace of Holyroodhouse. There is a copy of the register of those who took this step at RH.2/8/17-20. It is not indexed.

Photograph from Court of Session Process, c. 1916. (ex RH.19/15/3)

*C*riminals

12.1 It is an irony of ancestor-hunting that you are more likely to find information about an ancestor who committed a crime than one who was a respectable, law–abiding citizen. Such information may be found in records of the inquiries into the case, records of various criminal courts, and in prison records.

Precognitions

12.2 A precognition is the written report of the evidence of witnesses to a crime, taken before the trial to help prepare the case against the accused (whether or not he ever comes to trial). Precognitions for the more serious crimes are preserved among the Lord Advocate's records (AD). Hardly any survive before 1812. Up to 1900, the precognitions are referenced AD.14, and, from 1901, AD.15. The second number in each reference represents the year, eg an 1834 precognition will be numbered AD.14/34. They are catalogued within years, by the name of the accused, with full designation up to 1900. From 1901, only the name and the crime is stated in the catalogue. Here you will find records of labourers, servants, hawkers and others who leave little or no trace in property records.

Reference AD 14		
30/241	McDONALD, Ewen Son of Duncan McDonald, Flesher in Inverness	Stouthrief Theft by housebreaking
	MACBEAN, James (Junior) Son of James MacBean Shoemaker, in Inverness	Stouthrief Theft by housebreaking
30/242	DARLING, William Carter, Sand Port Street, North Leith	Theft - previous conviction
	FOSTER, George Recruit, 79th Regiment of Foot, Glasgow	Theft
30/243	EMOND, Robert Grocer & Draper, North Berwick	Murder
30/244	RENNIE, Jane or Jean Spence's Place, Canal Basin, Edinburgh	Falsehood, Fraud and Wilful Imposition
	KITCHEN, Ann o.a. Watt Widow of John Kitchen, Tailor Mid-common Close, Canongate, Edinburgh	Theft
30/245	GRANT, Daniel Printer, Blackfriars Wynd, High Street, Edinburgh	Theft of a body

List of 1830 precognitions in AD.14 repertory

12.3 If you believe that your ancestor was suspected of committing a crime between 1812 and 1900, look at the card index which repeats all the information in the AD.14 catalogue in alphabetical order of accused. You will find such entries as 'AD.14/34/373 Robertson, James, alias David Smith, alias James Burns, Cotton Spinner, Calton, Glasgow. Theft by housebreaking. Previous conviction.' Precognitions contain not only statements by the witnesses, but also a declaration by the accused. If you order out James Robertson's precognition, you will find that he declared that he was a native of Manchester, aged 26, had in 1826 committed a theft and been sentenced to transportation for seven years and had returned to Glasgow in 1833. (For this second offence, he was sentenced to transportation for life.) Crimes which led to a sentence of transportation are likely to be found among the Precognitions.

12.4 If the crime was committed after 1900, there is no index and you have to look through the AD.15 catalogue, year by year. Note that there is a 75-year closure of these precognitions.

12.5 Two other of the Lord Advocate's records provide useful reports of the progress of such criminal investigations. (They too are closed for 75 years.) From 1822, there are procedure books (AD.9), which are arranged, first by geographical areas, and then chronologically. They record the name (not designation) of the accused, the crime and whether the case was to be brought to trial or not and by what court. You will then know what court record to search for the details of the trial. Even more useful, but unfortunately dating only from 1890, is AD.8, a series of ledgers which record all criminal cases reported to the Crown Agent, giving the name (not designation) of the accused, details of the crime, date and place of the trial, the plea, verdict and sentence. The arrangement is by first letter of the accused's surname and then chronological.

High Court of Justiciary

12.6 Apart from the Precognitions after 1812, the principal source to search for information about a criminal ancestor is the records of the High Court of Justiciary, the supreme criminal court in Scotland. Its records, which are all open to public inspection, are listed in the JC repertory. The Court sat both in Edinburgh and on circuit in other parts of Scotland. If a crime was committed in the Edinburgh area, the case would be tried in Edinburgh. Otherwise, it might be tried either in Edinburgh or on circuit.

12.7 The records of the Edinburgh sittings are contained in the Books of Adjournal (JC.2-5) and minute books (JC.6 9). Both of these report the trials fully. There are modern indexes for the periods 1611-1631 and 1699-1720, and selected trials are published in Pitcairn's *Criminal Trials in Scotland, 1498-1624* (3 volumes, Bannatyne Club) and *Selected Justiciary Cases, 1624-50* (3 volumes, Stair Society).

12.8 Those apart, you will look for the name of an accused in bound xerox copies of manuscript chronological lists of cases heard by the High Court in

Edinburgh. These lists are inaccurately entitled as indexes. The accused is usually described as the 'Pannel', and may be noted only on his first appearance, though the trial may continue over several days. If there are several accused in one trial, only one may be named in the list. If you find the name of an accused who interests you, look at the Books of Adjournal and/or minute books for the date given. For example, we find on 5th January 1736, the pannel is 'Barrisdale' and the crime is 'subborning witnesses'. This, incidentally, illustrates one problem of these indexes in that 'Barrisdale' is not a surname but the name of the estate owned by the accused, who is Coll McDonell, younger of Barrisdale. You are interested in him and therefore you look at the record of his trial in JC.3/20 and JC.7/20, where you find it continues until 10 February, when he is acquitted.

12.9 If you suspect that your ancestor was accused of a crime and he does not appear in the above-mentioned lists, then it is possible that he was tried by the Court on circuit, which it did in the North, South and West. The records of the Court on circuit are minute books (JC.10- 14), which exist from 1655 and fully report the trials. From 1890, there are also Circuit Books of Adjournal (JC.15). To find a case up to 1830, you have to plough through a minute book at the likely date. To find a case between 1830 and 1887, look in the AD repertory and order out the AD.6 volume for the relevant date. The AD.6 volumes list all circuit cases, 1830–87, giving the name of the accused plus the verdict and sentence. If you find your man, you can then study his trial in the JC circuit minute book. From 1887 there are lists available in the Search Room of cases for each circuit court. Another record you may consult is the Circuit Books of Appeal (JC.22) which date from 1748 and record appeals from lower courts to the circuit courts. Again there is no index and you must just read through the record.

12.10 An alternative source of information about 19th- and 20th-century Justiciary Court cases may be found in the Lord Advocate's records. AD.2–5 consist of bound copies of printed indictments, which give full details of each accused and crime and list the witnesses for each trial. AD.2 has high court indictments, 1829-91, and AD.3 circuit court indictments, 1839-87, each volume including a contents list of names of accused. AD.4 contains indictments relating to postal offences, 1822-74. AD.5 contains miscellaneous high and circuit court indictments, 1837-43, with no contents list, but annotated with each verdict and sentence.

12.11 If your ancestor was transported as punishment for committing a crime, then the record of his trial should be in the JC records. Transportation ceased to be used as a punishment in 1857, but some prisoners sentenced to penal servitude were transported until 1867 (see 12.22).

Privy Council

12.12 Until 1707, criminal cases might also be dealt with by the Privy Council. To find such a case, follow the advice in 11.28-30.

Sheriff Courts

12.13 If your criminal ancestor was not tried in the High Court, the next most likely court to have judged him is the sheriff court (see list at 11.36). The commonest crimes to be tried there were theft and assault. Assuming that you know where your ancestor was in Scotland, look in the contents list of the repertory of the records of the relevant sheriffdom(s) for the Criminal Court records. The criminal records of the various sheriff courts bear various titles and commence at widely varying dates. The main record, reporting the trials, may be called 'Criminal Court Books', 'Criminal Record', 'Criminal Register', 'Record of Criminal Trials', etc. The only indexes are within some of the volumes of the record themselves. These supply only surname and Christian name and only at the first appearance. In some sheriff courts, there are separate records of trials heard by the sheriff with a jury and those heard by the sheriff sitting alone. If there are no criminal court records for the years you are searching, try the ordinary court records, which sometimes report both civil and criminal cases. Check also in the repertory for criminal libels and/or indictments, as these sometimes survive from an earlier date than the court record. These may include various relative papers, such as a declaration by the accused. For instance, in 1828, the sheriff court of Lanark investigated a charge against one John Anderson for passing forged bank notes. His declaration shows that he was a pedlar, about 19 years of age, usually residing in Castle Douglas, born in Girvan, where his father resided, and was bred a weaver (sc.38/55/1).

Franchise Courts

12.14 Minor offences were usually tried in local courts. Until 1747, such offenders might be brought before one of the 'franchise' courts, which are described in 11.49-51. As criminal courts, they heard such cases as assault ('blood and ryot') and scandal and illegal fishing. Occasionally, such a court dealt with a serious offence, eg in 1666 James Cramond was banished from the town of Kelso for theft (RH.11/42/1). In the administration of such courts, there was no practical distinction made between civil and criminal cases, which are intermingled in the court books.

12.15 A unique franchise court was the Argyll Justiciary Court which had criminal jurisdiction throughout Argyll and the Western Isles. Its records, which date from 1664 to 1742, have been published in the *Argyll Justiciary Records* (Stair Society) in two volumes, which are indexed. The reference numbers of the originals of these records are sc.51/40/1-4.

Burgh Courts

12.16 Minor offences within royal burghs would be tried by the burgh court. Again, the records of such trials are intermingled in the court books with the other business of the court. (See 11.48.) Most offences tried by a burgh court were of the nature of a breach of a peace, but their records have a particular genealogical value in that these courts fined the participants in irregular marriages. For example, in Peebles in 1728, James Montgomery, cripple, for the present residing in Peebles, and Jean Drysdale were fined by the magistrates for their irregular marriage by the vicar of Irthington (in Cumberland) on 8th March 1726. Jean Drysdale was later banished from the burgh for another offence (B.58/9/4).

Justice of Peace Courts

12.17 See 11.47 for how to search the JP records. The JP courts also had a criminal jurisdiction. The records in the court books are usually brief and the offences charged vary from court to court. In country areas, the commonest crime was pursuit of game (ie poaching). In towns, the offences were more varied - theft, scandal, riot, breach of peace, being a whore. Occasionally, people were fined for irregular marriage or witnessing one. For example, in 1728, Antony Aston, comedian in Edinburgh, was fined for being witness to his son Walter's irregular marriage with Mrs Jean Kerr (JP.35/4/2).

Admiralty Court

12.18 If your ancestor committed a crime on the high seas up to 1830, then the record of his trial may be among the Admiralty Court records. In the AC repertory, look up AC.16, which lists the volumes which contain the reports of these trials. They date from 1705. There is no index, but each volume has a contents list. Very few cases were in fact heard by the Admiralty Court.

Witnesses

12.19 The depositions of witnesses are a hidden genealogical source among records of criminal trials, hidden and often inaccessible because any indexing or listing is done by name of the accused, and you may never know that your ancestor was a witness to a crime. Yet when a witness gave evidence, his age, marital status, trade and place of abode were all recorded. Such depositions are found most commonly in the Precognitions and the High Court of Justiciary records. Here are two examples. From a precognition, 1834 - 'John McDonald, aged fourteen, son of, and residing with Dougal McDonald, Porter at the Broomilaw, Glasgow' (AD.14/34/373). From a trial record, 1736 - 'Evan More McAphie alias Cameron formerly in Shian in Glengarry parish of Kilmanivage and shire of Inverness now in Kilin in the shire of Perth aged 52 years or thereby married' (JC.7/20).

Prisoners

12.20 Persons accused of crimes might, before the trial, be lodged in prison, as well as finding themselves there after sentence, either for a period of imprisonment or while waiting for transportation or hanging. Personal information about prisoners may be found in those prison registers which are preserved among the Home and Health Department records (HH).

12.21 Check the HH.21 lists in the HH repertory to see if there is a register of
prisoners in a prison in which your ancestor might have been placed. Many
of these registers only cover the 1840s to the 1870s. Some continue into the
20th century and are closed for 75 years. Remember that, until 1880, civil
debtors as well as those charged with or found guilty of crimes might be
imprisoned. If the register is only of criminal prisoners, this is specified in the
repertory. Most of these registers supply the name, age, height, marital status,
places of birth and residence, occupation and religion of each prisoner, as well
as his crime, the court which tried him and the sentence.

12.22 Information about prisoners who were sentenced to transportation may be
found in the register of a prison which served the court where they were tried,
or in the registers of prisons in Aberdeen and Edinburgh where such prisoners
waited to be moved to England. The records of the Edinburgh (Calton) Prison
include a separate register of convicts under sentence of transportation from
1852 (HH.21/5/16). This provides the name, age, crime, place of trial, marital
status and trade of each prisoner, along with comments by the chaplain. As the
ships which carried such prisoners to Australia sailed from England, further
information about them is kept in the Home Office records in the Public
Record Office in London. These Home Office records include convict
transportation registers, 1787-1870, of which you may consult a microfilm copy
in the SRO (RH.4/160). These registers are arranged chronologically by date of
departure of each ship. The last microfilm reel (RH.4/160/7) includes a list of
ships to each colony and an index of ships, showing the date and destination of
each. The Scots prisoners are placed near the end of the list of convicts on each
ship. The information given is the name of the convict and where, when and
for how many years he was sentenced. There could be a delay of several years
between conviction and transportation. The last transportation ship to sail to
Western Australia in 1867 carried Alex Casey, who had been sentenced to 15
years penal servitude in Edinburgh in 1858.

12.23 Outwith the HH.21 series, there are two further sets of prison registers of
particular interest. HH.11 is the reference number of the Edinburgh Tolbooth
Warding and Liberation Books, 1657-1816. These 39 volumes usually have a
contents list under initial letters of surnames. They deal with both civil and
criminal prisoners, stating their name and designation, at whose instance they
are incarcerated and sometimes which court dealt with the case. Extracts from
these records, 1657-1686, have been published in the *Book of the Old Edinburgh
Club*, volumes 4-6, 8, 9, 11, 12. The Liberation information may occasionally
be of further use. For example, in October 1735, William Fowler, an Irishman,
was incarcerated by a warrant of his employers, a firm of shipbuilders in Irvine,
for theft. Three weeks later, he was liberated by warrant both of his employers
and of the JPs 'who Indented with Mr Ferguson for the plantations,'
(HH.11/18).

12.24 HH.12 is a series of miscellaneous prison records, including records of prisoners
in the condemned cell. The most valuable record in the series is a bound set
of forms giving particulars of prisoners in Greenock Prisons, 1872-1888

12-year-old prisoners in Greenock gaol, 1873. (HH.12/56/7)

(HH.12/56/7). Not only do these forms supply detailed personal information about each prisoner, but added is a photograph of the prisoner in his or her best clothes.

Pardons and Remissions

12.25 A few criminals have the fortune to have their crime pardoned or their sentence remitted. Such remissions, often reducing a sentence of death to that of transportation, were granted by the Crown through the office of the Great Seal. If you are looking for a remission granted before 1668, use the published *Register of the Great Seal of Scotland* (see 8.23-25) and *Register of the Privy Seal of Scotland* (see 5.17). There is a modern typed index of remissions between 1668 and 1906. This supplies the name, sometimes designation, place of conviction and offence of each person, with the date of remission and volume and running number (not page number) of the Great Seal Paper Register. If you find your ancestor in this index, order out by c.3 and the volume number, unless the volume number is preceded by a letter (eg S32), in which case refer to the introduction to the index for fresh advice. The index includes some remissions omitted from the Great Seal Register but surviving in other records. Remissions are granted for a wide variety of crimes, adultery and drunkenness as well as murder. In 1896, William Cochrane was remitted his five shilling fine by the Glasgow Police Court for playing football on the street (c.3/47, no 64). Until 1896, these remissions are in Latin. However, they do not contain much information not in the index, never explaining why the remission was granted, but may be useful in leading you to the court records of the case. English versions of remissions between 1762 and 1849 may be found in RH.2/4/255-273, which are photostat copies of the Home Office Criminal Entry Books for Scotland (originals in the Public Record Office).

$\mathscr{T}$axpayers

13.1 Tax records have already been mentioned in respect of death duties (6.31-32) and land tax (8.38-40), which was also known as the cess.

13.2 Various other types of taxes were levied for varying periods of years. The lists of people liable for each tax or of payments made by them may be worth examining. At least, you may find that a person of a certain name was resident in a certain parish.

Hearth Tax

13.3 In 1690, Parliament granted a tax on every hearth in the kingdom. Both landowners and tenants were liable to pay and therefore may be named in the records of this tax, which date between 1691 and 1695, but have not all survived. Look at the repertory referenced E.69 and read the introduction thereto. The records are arranged by counties. Within a county, look for a List of hearths or, not quite so useful, Accounts of hearth money collected (these may omit personal names). If you order out a list or account for your county, you will find it is arranged by parishes. Within parishes, there will be a list of those who had hearths in their houses, eg 'Georg Edgar tennent in Evelaw three [hearths], John Wilson coatter there one' (E.69/5/1). Sometimes just the name of the hearth-owner is given, without designation. There is a supplementary series of hearth tax records for the same period in the Leven and Melville Muniments. Look up the GD.26 inventory at references GD.26/7/300-391. Lists of hearths in some Ross-shire parishes are in the Cromartie Muniments (GD.305/1/64, nos 240-1, 243, 271 2, 277, 280-1).

Poll Tax

13.4 Poll taxes were imposed on Scotland between 1693 and 1699 on all adults except those dependent on charity. Unfortunately, the records are not complete. Look in the repertory referenced E.70. This lists two series of records, each arranged by counties, the E.70 series itself and a supplementary list of poll-tax records surviving in other record groups. This latter list also notes some printed versions. Having read the introduction, look at both lists under the relevant county. These describe assorted lists and accounts of pollable

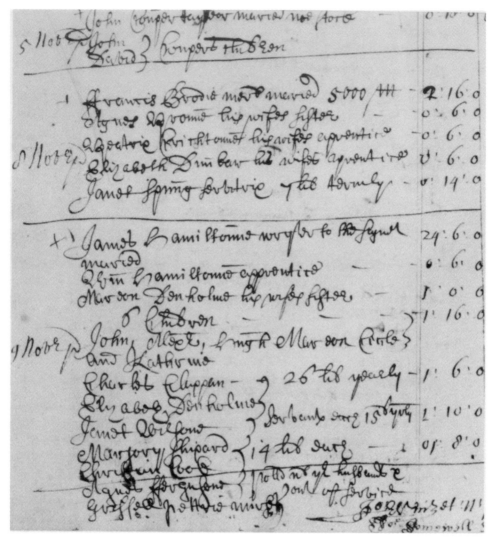

Excerpt from Edinburgh poll tax record, 1694. (E.70/4/5)

persons, the information, which is variable, again collected within parishes. At their most informative, these records can be genealogically useful, naming children and servants, eg 'James Rutherfurde Tennent in Sawchtan for himself, his wife, Wm, Janet and Eliza[t] his children' (E.70/8/1 – Account for parish of Crichton in Midlothian).

Post-Union Taxes

13.5   From 1748, certain assessed taxes were levied in Scotland and copies of the lists (schedules) of people assessed to pay have been preserved among the Exchequer records. Look at the E.326 repertory and read first the general introduction and the introductions to the individual tax records. The records of each tax are arranged by counties, as described in the repertory, and within counties by parishes (not in alphabetical order), but royal burghs are listed separately - check the repertory carefully.

13.6 Window Tax, 1748-1798(E.326/1),Commutation Tax, 1784-1798 (E.326/2), Inhabited House Tax, 1778-1798 (E.326/3) and Consolidated Assessed Taxes, 1798-1799 (E.326/15) were all taxes on householders (owners or tenants, one per dwelling house). However, this record is not as useful as it sounds, as only the better-off were taxed. A house had to have at least seven windows or a rent of at least £5 yearly before it was liable for tax. In some rural parishes, the only persons liable for tax were the minister and a couple of lairds. The schedules for burghs and some more populous parishes are useful in listing more names, but omission of designations and of locations of the dwelling houses limits their usefulness. The schedule for the burgh of Aberdeen in 1773 lists 546 window-tax-paying inhabitants, but they include five ladies described simply as 'Mrs Forbes' (E326/1/128).

13.7 A shop tax was levied between 1785 and 1789. If you want to find if your ancestor had a retail shop worth a rental of more than £5 per year at that time, look at E.326/4. Unfortunately, the retail business is not always specified.

13.8 Taxes were levied on certain classes of servants, mainly domestic (male servants, 1777-1798, E.326/5, and female, 1785-1792, E.326/6). While you may want to find out how many servants your well-off ancestor employed, the schedules of these taxes are more significant in that they usually name the servants, sometimes also stating what kind of servant, and in that the record notes which masters were bachelors as they had to pay double tax. In Earlston parish in 1778, Captain Colin Falconer's footman was 'Osemin a Negro' (E.326/5/1).

13.9 The other assessed taxes, on carts, carriages, horses, dogs and clocks and watches, all for brief periods of years up to 1798, are, with one exception, of little added use. The exception is Farm Horse Tax (1797-1798, E.326/10) which is continued in the Consolidated Assessed Taxes (1798-1799, E.326/15). Its value is that it helps to identify tenant farmers. In the parish of Strathdon in 1799, three persons paid window-tax, five more paid house tax, but another 47 paid farm horse tax (E.326/15/1). It is unfortunate that this record covers such a short period of time, being continued only for Midlothian up to 1812 (E.327/36-54).

13.10 Income tax was first imposed in 1799 on annual incomes of £60 and over. Lists of those who made returns survive for Midlothian, 1799-1801 (E.327/18-31), and for certain other counties and burghs (see the repertory) for 1801-1802 (F.326/14). One point of interest here is that abatements were made on account of children. If the number of children is not stated, it should be possible to calculate how many from the sum deducted. The rules for such abatements are contained in the Duties on Income Act, 1778.

13.11 Income tax was replaced in 1803 by a property tax assessed on income from ownership and occupation of land, investments, trades and offices. The Exchequer records contain records for Midlothian only, 1803–1812 (E.327/78–121). The trades and offices of tax-payers are specified, particularly in Edinburgh, where the arrangement is by street within parish. Natale Corri at the Concert Hall was assessed as making a profit in 1803 of £200 from his trade as a musician (E. 327/81).

$\mathcal{G}$overnment Officials

14.1 The highest-ranking government officials are listed in the *Handbook of British Chronology* (Royal Historical Society, London). The appointments of slightly less high ranking officials may be found in the records of the Great and Privy Seal: officials such as sheriffs and other judges, lieutenants of counties, keepers of registers of sasines, sheriff and commissary clerks. Indexes of such commissions, both of persons and of offices, are available from 1668 to 1955 (Great Seal) and from 1660 to 1898 (Privy Seal, English record). Most of these Great Seal commissions are ordered out by the reference c.3 and the volume number, but not all – first check the introductory pages to the index. Privy Seal commissions are ordered out by ps.3 and the volume number. For earlier commissions, you should use the printed Great and Privy Seal volumes, except for the Privy Seal record between 1585 and 1660 when you should use a list referenced ps.7/1 which leads you to the entries in volumes referenced ps.1. If your ancestor is unexpectedly absent from these records or you want more information about his appointment, try the records mentioned in 14.2-3.

14.2 Lists of the holders of some of these minor offices (including HM Limner, the Historiographer-Royal and Governors of Edinburgh Castle) are available in the Historical Search Room (library reference 334). Adjacent on the shelf is a typed volume (library reference 332) 'Civil and Judicial Establishment 1707-1830'. This is a copy of an Exchequer record (e.229/10/1) which lists the holders of various offices, including the staffs of the Courts of Exchequer, Justiciary and Session. Unfortunately, this record is incomplete.

14.3 Government officials had to be paid and, as a result, post-Union bureaucracy produced several series of Exchequer records, which give information of the appointments and salaries of officials after 1707. These records overlap considerably and are not consistent throughout each series. It is not overtly apparent why information may be in one record and not another. The following are the most useful and are all in volume form. Look at the relevant repertory for dates and call numbers of each volume. In these volumes there are indexes or contents lists of commissions and warrants, but no indexes of the persons named in the salary lists. Some also contain records of other payments, including Civil List pensions (ie annuities to worthy persons in need), so that you may find there an ancestor who received an income from the government, even if not employed by them: but look first at the index to the Privy Seal English Record (PS.3) for such pensioners.

E.313   Copies of commissions and warrants for paying salaries etc, 1709-1965.

E.224   Establishment entry books containing lists of salaries and pensions, 1709-1866, and warrants thereof, 1709-1834. Judges and court officials will be found throughout: later volumes include staffs of government boards and of Register House. The last list in which a person appears will often provide the date on which he died or left office.

E.810   Lists of salaries, superannuations, and pensions, 1854-1930. Useful range of recipients.

E.811   Lists of salaries, 1869-1930. Include staffs of the Exchequer, court offices, Register House, boards and commissions.

14.4 A government employee may of course be mentioned in the records of the department in which he was employed and therefore it may be worth checking establishment or staff records in the repertory of that department's records. For example, if your ancestor was employed in the General Register Office between 1909 and 1920, he should appear in the files referenced GRO.5/774-776. However, in most of these departmental records, records of staff do not start until well into the 20th century and do not include personal files. The staff of three government organisations before 1900 are, however, well recorded – the Board of Customs, the Board of Excise, and the Post Office.

14.5 A separate Scottish Board of Customs functioned from 1707 until 1829. Look in the CE repertory at CE.3 and CE.12 for establishment books. These contain quarterly lists, arranged by port, of all Customs officers, except junior clerks and the crews of cutters (commanders and mates are named). Payments of salaries to Customs officers are recorded in the Customs cash accounts (E.502). The date payment stopped would be the date of death, dismissal or resignation. If your ancestor was a Customs officer in the mid-18th century, look at two further records, GD.1/372/1 and RH.2/8/102 which list the officers in 1752 and 1755, arranged by port and supplying for each his age and character (eg 'A tipler, Indolent, & not capable' or 'Capable & Sober. Worn out in the Service'). GD.1/372/1 valuably also records his birthplace, if he has a wife and how many children.

14.6 The separate Scottish Board of Excise survived until 1830. Its records are also listed in the CE repertory. Mr J F Mitchell gathered information about the Excise officers between 1707 and 1830 from this and other sources and noted it on cards arranged alphabetically. These cards may be consulted in the SRO on microfilm (RH.4/6/1-2). The information is supplied in rather succinct form, and therefore you should first read the explanation of the arrangement of the symbols on the cards which appears at the beginning of the microfilm. Although Mitchell searched widely, the information on his cards is not exclusive. You may find further details, or simply prefer to search first, in

GD.1/54/10, which includes a list of Excise officers in 1743; CE.6/19, which lists all officers in 1794 under the initial letter of each's surname, stating his age and the number of his family; or CE.13/1-9, which is a series of volumes minuting the appointments and removals of Excise staff between 1813 and 1829. The CE.13 volumes are indexed by initial letter of surnames, then by order of appearance in the book.

14.7 The Post Office records contain a series of establishment books, listing the salaried staff, from 1803 to 1911 (PO.1/15-65). These books are arranged by post-towns, naming all the staff in the main post offices, including letter carriers, but do not name sub-postmasters. PO.1/16, which records postal staff in 1803, notes their dates of appointment (eg Margaret MacKerchar was appointed to Aberfeldy in 1799) and also has later annotations.

15

*S*oldiers and Sailors

15.1 After 1707, the Army and Navy were administered from London. Therefore, if you are seeking information about the military or naval service of an ancestor after 1707, you should apply to the Public Record Office which holds the War Office and Admiralty records. Even before the Union, references in the records to named individuals in the Scottish army and navy are sparse (particularly the navy). Nevertheless, there are records in the SRO which may be of use to you. Further to those described below, you should look at the source lists of military records and naval and mercantile records.

Soldiers before 1707

15.2 The main record of individuals in the Scottish army is the Muster Rolls which are in the Exchequer records. Look at the repertory referenced E.100. These muster rolls are arranged by regiment and, within regiment, by companies or troops. Though the earliest is dated 1641, most are dated after 1680. They name all the officers and men in a troop or company at a certain place and date. Ranks are stated, except for troopers. Few rolls supply any other information. Your problem is that unless you already know that your ancestor was in a particular regiment, you may have to look through some 4,800 rolls in the hope of finding him. It may help you that many recruits came from the estates owned by their Colonel or his family and most regiments were known by the name of their commanding officer (eg Lord Jedburgh's dragoons). Some of these rolls are printed in *The Scots Army, 1661-1688* by C Dalton (republished in 1989 by Greenhill Books), but only officers appear in the book's index. Similar lists of those serving in particular regiments may be found in GD collections (see 4.18-19), where a member of that family had been granted a commission to be Colonel of a regiment.

15.3 If your ancestor was an officer, there is more likely to be a record of him, than if he was a common soldier. Commissions in the army were granted by the Crown and, from 1670, some were recorded in the Warrant Books of the Secretary of Scotland, along with other government business. Look up the State Papers repertory at SP.4 to find the volume covering the relevant dates. These volumes each contain a contents list or index. The commissions supply only the name, rank, company and regiment of the officer, no other personal details. These SP.4 commissions are noted and indexed in Dalton's *The Scot's*

Army, 1661-1688 and thereafter in his *English Army Lists and Commission Registers, 1661-1714*. There is also a small series of commissions, 1643, 1689-1827, in RH.9/9 - look up that repertory; and commissions may occasionally be found in GD collections.

Soldiers after 1707

15.4 The only military records after the Union among public records in the SRO are those of the Militia and more recently the Territorials.

15.5 Though Militia records run from the 1790s to mid-19th-century, the heyday of the Militia force was the Napoleonic Wars. These records have two main points of genealogical interest: they name the young men who were balloted to serve in the Militia and they name some of their wives. Look in the repertory of Sheriff Court (SC) or County Council (CO) records of the sheriffdom or county in which your ancestor lived. The relevant records, if they survive, will be catalogued under the heading of Lieutenancy and/or Militia or Miscellaneous. They usually appear near the end of an SC repertory. A list of references to militia records is printed in J Gibson and M Medlycott's *Militia Lists and Musters 1757-1876* (Federation of Family History Societies, 1994).

15.6 As conscription was by ballot, only some men were made to serve. The militiamen had to be healthy and between 18 and 30, until 1802, thereafter between 18 and 45. Certain categories were exempted, including apprentices and poor men with more than two children (see the Militia (Scotland) Act 1802 (s.38)). Despite these limitations, the Militia records name many people whose existence might not otherwise be recorded. In the Highland parish of Braemar and Crathie in 1800, 60 young men were listed (CO.6/5/6). Information about individual militiamen appears in the schedules of those eligible to be balloted (some claiming exemption), in lists of men conscripted, and in minute books. The basic information supplied about a militiaman is his name, profession and place of abode, but sometimes his age is stated and, more rarely, place of birth. Thus we know that Charles Herkes aged 22, a weaver in Dunbar in 1825, was born in County Down (CO. 7/13/2).

15.7 When a man was serving in the Militia and his family were unable to support themselves, his wife and children under 10 years of age were eligible for an allowance. Records of claims for such allowances appear among Lieutenancy and Militia records. These name each wife and, usually but not invariably, her husband; say how many children, sometimes naming them; and state the parish where she lived. An additional record of such payments to wives and children in Midlothian, 1803-1815, is contained in the Exchequer records (E.327/147-158).

15.8 Some militia records may be found in the GD series (see 4.18-19). For example, the Seaforth Muniments include lists of men between 15 and 60 able to bear arms in parishes in Ross-shire in 1798 (GD.46/6/45).

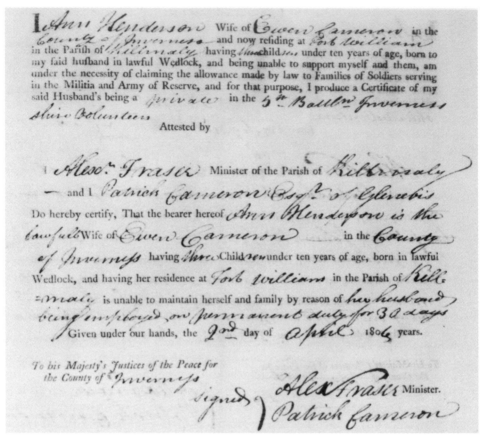

Application by wife of militiaman for financial support, 1805. (SC.29/72/2)

15.9 The Ministry of Defence records in the SRO consist of Territorial and Auxiliary Forces Associations' records. These include a list of members of Dundee Volunteer Rifle Corps in 1859 (MD.7/1), a muster roll of the 5th Forfarshire Volunteer Corps 1859–1886 (MD.7/2) which gives the ages, occupations and residences of the volunteers, and a list of members of the Dundee National Reserve in 1914 (MD.7/3). The rest of the MD records are all post 1900 and mostly minute books. While officers are regularly named in them, other ranks are rarely named.

Sailors

15.10 There are no official records of the Scottish navy, as such. There are a few miscellaneous naval documents in the Exchequer records: see list E.90. The most useful of these are printed in *The Old Scots Navy, 1689-1710* by James Grant. Those apart, information about Scottish ships and the men who sailed in them has to be gleaned from the various records of Scottish government, such as the Privy Council.

Merchant Seamen

15.11 Though both before and after 1707 the Customs Accounts record the movement of ships in and out of ports, they do not record the names of crew or passengers. Only the master or captain of the ship is named. These Customs Accounts are referenced E.71 (for the period up to 1640), E.72 (1662-1696) and E.504 (1742-1830). They are arranged by ports.

15.12 The crews of ships engaged in whale-fishing between1750 and 1825 are named in the vouchers of payments of bounties (E.508/47/8-130/8). The ships, ports and owners are named in the Customs cash accounts (E.502/ 48-130), which provide a key to the individual vouchers. Similarly, the crews of ships engaged in herring-fishing between 1752 and 1796 are named in the more numerous vouchers for herring bounties (E.508/49/9-96/9). Here again the cash accounts (E.502) record ships, owners and ports, which should lead you to the voucher you want.

15.13 Seamen who used the port of Leith may be found in the records of Trinity House of Leith (GD.226), a mutual benefit society for the support of the poor, aged and infirm mariners and their dependents. Minute and cash books date from the mid-17th-century and record payments by seamen as well as pensions to them and their dependents, mainly widows. Included are records of the pilots who guided ships into the harbour.

15.14 Since 1835, it has been compulsory for masters of ships to enter into agreements with any crew member before sailing. Not all records of such agreements have been kept. A small number, dating between 1867 and 1913 and relating to Scottish ships, are preserved in the SRO. Look up the repertory referenced BT.3. If this record fails you, you should try the crew lists in the Glasgow City Archives, the Public Record Office, the National Maritime Museum in London and the Memorial University, Newfoundland. These crew agreements supply the name, age and birthplace of each seaman. To search this record, you need to know the name of the ship in which your ancestor might have sailed.

16

*C*lergymen and Church Members

Presbyterian Ministers

16.1 If your ancestor was a Presbyterian clergyman who had a parish or congregation, then look for him in one of the following printed sources.

*Fasti Ecclesiae Scoticanae.*This series of volumes provides biographical, including family, details of all known ministers of the established Church of Scotland since the Reformation. Some omissions from early volumes are corrected in volume 8. As much of the information in the *Fasti* was based on record research, it may be worth following up references given in particular biographies.

History of the Congregations of the United Presbyterian Church, 1733-1900

*Annals and Statistics of the Original Secession Church.*This book is not indexed.

Annals of the Free Church of Scotland, 1843-1900

The Fasti of the United Free Church of Scotland, 1900-1929

These last four publications contain information about the main denominations which dissented from the Church of Scotland in the 18th and 19th centuries. Additional details will be found in the records of the churches and presbyteries in which these men served (see CH repertories). Information about some dissenting ministers may be found in their Friendly Society records (CH.3/515-517). CH.3/515/8, a list of Relief Synod ministers, gives the dates of birth, marriage and death of them and their wives.

16.2 One can search for divinity students in the minutes of the presbyteries and synods (CH.2 and 3) in which they were probationers. Some are mentioned briefly in the mainly 19th century records of theological colleges and student societies (CH.3/119, CH.3/273, CH.3/281, CH.3/305, CH.3/885).

16.3 It may be difficult to find a record of a Presbyterian clergyman who did not succeed in obtaining a church in Scotland. Some, between 1725 and 1876, may have been appointed itinerant preachers and catechists within the Highlands and Islands and, as such, appear in the records of the Royal Bounty Committee of the General Assembly of the Church of Scotland (CH.1/5/51-79). These records are unindexed but include marginal tags and occasional lists of the catechists. Some missionaries and catechists had their salaries paid by the Society in Scotland for Propagating Christian Knowledge (see 17.6) and are named in the SSPCK's scheme ledgers (GD.95/7). Records of Presbyterian missionaries abroad are preserved in the National Library of Scotland.

Other Clergymen

16.4 In the absence of published biographical details, information about non-Presbyterian clergymen must be found in the records of their churches (try the CH repertories) or by enquiring of their present-day church headquarters.

16.5 Roman Catholic secular clergy, 1732-1878, are listed in *The Innes Review* (Scottish Catholic Historical Association), volumes 17, 34 and 40. Registers of student priests at the Scots Colleges at Douai, Rome, Madrid, Valladolid and Ratisbon are printed and indexed in *Records of Scots Colleges* (New Spalding Club, 1906). The information is in Latin, but often includes the age and parentage of the student. The SRO has a photocopy of the register of the College in Rome 1602-1939 (RH.2/7/14) and a microfilm copy of the registers of the College at Douai 1581-1772 (RH.4/18). Further enquiries about Roman Catholic priests might be made to the Scottish Catholic Archives (address in Appendix A).

Presbyterian Church Members

16.6 Not until the mid-19th-century did it become common for the church records to include lists of church members ('communicants') or to record the names of those who joined that church. Such information is sometimes contained in separate volumes - look in the list of records of the church in question in the CH repertory for a communion roll, list of communicants, list of parishioners, roll of male heads of families, etc. Such lists sometimes tell if a communicant came from another parish. Lists of communicants are sometimes inscribed in the kirk session minute books, particularly lists of young communicants on their joining the Kirk. The names of those who rented seats in a church may appear in account books.

16.7 In 17th- and 18th-century kirk session records, you will find the names of elders, those in receipt of poor relief, and those accused of or witness to scandalous behaviour (most commonly fornication, but it could be shoeing a horse on the Sabbath). Otherwise parishioners are not usually named, even when they move into the parish. But one cannot be categorical about this: for example, the earliest minute book of Linlithgow kirk session (CH.2/740/1) records testimonials brought by incomers to the parish, 1645-1647.

List of papists within the presbytery of Kirkcudbright given in by the bookroom of the presbetrie upon the 16 may 1704 and transmitted by the sd presbry to the clerks of her majesties most Honrable privie Councell

List of papists in the parroch of Buittle

John Maxuel of Brakenside excomunicat
John Davison his servant appostat
Barbara Maxuel relict of the deceast
Gorge Maxuel of Munchees appostat
Margret Smith her servant
George Maxuel of Munchees
Kathrine Maxuel his spouse
William Maxuel his son about 18 years of age now in france
George Maxuel his son about 14 years of age now in france
James Maxuel his son about 8 years of age
Barbara Maxuel his daughter about 12 years of age
Kathrine Maxuel his daughter about 10 years of age
John mc Girr servant to the sd George Maxuel appostat
Mary Smith his servant
Margret Wilson his servant
Margret Tait his servant
Robert Maxuel of Milltoune
Frances Maxuel of Broock
Mary Maxuel his spouse
Margret Maxuel his daughter about 6 years of age
Barbara Maxuel spouse to Alexr Maxuel of Balmangan
Edward Wilson woodseller of Burntstick
Robert Wilson his son about 8 years of age
Anna Wilson his daughter about 4 years of age
Alexander Wilson his son about 2 years of age
Robert Groocie tennant in Cooles appostat
Janet Laurie his spouse
James Groocie his son about 14 years of age
John Groocie his son about 12 years of age

Agnes Groocie his daughter about 20 years of age
Margret Groocie his daughter about 10 years of age
Thomas Coupland cottar in Munchees appostat
Agnes Thomson his spouse appost
George Coupland his son about ... years of age
William Coupland his son about ... years of age
John Coupland his son about ... years of age
Janet Coupland his daughter about 20 years of age
Margret Coupland his daughter about 13 years of age
Thomas Coupland his son about 10 years of age
George Coupland cottar in Munchees
Mary Wilis his spouse
William Coupland his son about 10 years of age
James Coupland his son about 7 years of age
Janet Coupland his daughter about 13 years of age
Barbara Coupland his daughter about 5 years of age
George Porter cottar in the Munchees
Elvi Wilson his spouse
Janet Porter her daughter about 12 years of age
Alexander Porter his son about 10 years of age
John Porter his son about 5 years of age
James Wilson cottar in the Munchees
Marion Lineurda his spouse appost
James Wilson his son
Agnes Wilson his daughter
James Corbie cottar in the Munchees
Isobel Corbie his spouse appost

turne over

List of Roman Catholics in parish of Buittle, 1704. (CH.1/2/5/3, no. 197/1)

Roman Catholics

16.8 Between 1700 and 1714, the names of Roman Catholics in their parishes were noted by each parish minister and these lists of 'papists' are preserved among the records of the General Assembly of the Church of Scotland. Look in the CH repertory at CH.1/2/5 and CH.1/2/29-34 for the reference numbers of lists of papists in the parishes in which your ancestors dwelt.

16.9 For more recent members of the Roman Catholic faith, look at the index of churches at the start of the RH.21 repertory and then at the records of a relevant church to see if they include a register of communicants or confirmations. The earliest of these date from 1749, but the majority are 19th century.

Members of Other Churches

16.10 Look at the CH repertory to see if the records of a particular church are in the SRO. Check the list of these records to see if they include a roll of members or communion roll: failing which look at minutes or other records. Note among the Episcopalian records lists of communicants in the dioceses of Ross, Caithness and Argyll in 1762 and 1770 (CH.12/1/12).

$\int$choolmasters and Scholars

17.1 The Education (Scotland) Act, 1872, was a watershed in the history of schooling in Scotland. The records which you should investigate for teachers are in the main different before and after that Act, though the ones mentioned in 17.6, 17.8 and 17.10 overlap 1872 to some extent. As there are many books about individual schools or education in particular areas and many of the relevant records are preserved in the region or district where the school was, you should first investigate the sources in the local library or record office. Within the SRO, look also at the three source lists on education. Source list no. 17 is incomplete but will refer you to relevant records in some GD collections. To trace your schoolmaster's name in the records suggested below will often involve searching unindexed minute books, some of which will have helpful marginal annotations (eg 'Ja: Turnbull schoolmaster'), some not.

Schoolmasters until 1872

17.2 The majority of schoolmasters taught in the parish or burgh school. You will find appointments of burgh schoolmasters recorded in the burgh or town council minutes. Look up the name of the burgh in the index to the B repertory, and in the list of records of that burgh look for the council minutes. For example, in 1690 the council of the burgh of Dunbar nominated James Turnbull, youngest lawful son to the deceased George Turnbull, merchant burgess of that burgh, to be schoolmaster 'for learning the Childrein to read, wryt, lay compts and work arthmetick' (B.18/13/2, f. 34v).

17.3 Parish schoolmasters were nominated by the heritors (ie landowners) and minister of the parish and usually were then examined by the presbytery to ensure that they were qualified for the post. The record of the appointment of a parish schoolmaster should be in the Heritors Records. Look up the name of the parish in the index to the HR repertory, and in the list of records for that parish look for the heritors' minutes. If no heritors' records survive for the required parish and date, then you should search the CH.2 records of that parish and the relevant presbytery. The kirk session records for the parish may contain the name of a schoolmaster, particularly as the schoolmaster often acted as session clerk. The presbytery minute books should record the presbytery's confirmation of the appointment of a schoolmaster. In the Church of Scotland, a presbytery is the court superior to the kirk session.

The *Fasti Ecclesiae Scoticanae* (see 16.1) will tell you which presbytery includes the parish in which you are interested.

17.4 The kirks of the Free Church of Scotland, which was founded in 1843, often set up their own schools. To find the record of the appointment of a teacher of a Free Church school, look up the name of the kirk in the CH.3 repertory and then the list of that kirk's records. Order out the Deacons Court minutes (rather than the Session minutes) as the deacons appointed and paid the teacher.

17.5 Schoolmasters may appear in other records. The records of a parliamentary commission in 1690 include some lists of schoolmasters. Those in the counties of Angus, Berwickshire, East Lothian, Fife, Midlothian, Peebleshire, Perthshire, Roxburghshire and Stirlingshire (PA.10./2) are printed in the Scottish History Society 4th series volume 2 *Miscellany X*. There is a list for Ayrshire among papers referenced PA.10/5.

17.6 Paradoxically, concern at the scarcity of schools in the Highlands and Islands led to a better recording of the schoolmasters who taught there. In the 18th and 19th centuries, the Society in Scotland for Propagating Christian Knowledge erected and maintained schools in the Highlands, Islands and Remote Corners of Scotland where 'popery and ignorance' did 'much abound'. Look at the inventory of their records which are referenced GD.95. While the Society's minute books, letter books and inspectors' reports mention teachers, you will find the names of the SSPCK teachers more quickly in the register of schools, 1710-1761 (GD.95/9/1); salary books, 1766-1779 (GD.95/8/5); scheme ledgers, 1771-1890 (GD.95/7); and abstract of school returns, 1827-1878 (GD.95/9/6-7). Some of these records are arranged by presbyteries.

17.7 The SSPCK appointed its own teachers, to supplement the parish school-masters appointed by the heritors. There are three other records which provide further information about the parish schoolmasters in the Highlands and Islands. The Commissioners who until 1784 administered the estates forfeited after the 1745 Jacobite rising were heritors of the parishes in which these estates lay and therefore the records of their administration includes the names of schoolmasters. There is a location list of the estates by county and parish at the beginning of the repertory of their records (E.700-788). Look up 'schools' in the index to the repertory and also look at the various reports on particular estates (E. 729 etc), some of which are printed (and indexed) in *Reports on the Annexed Estates, 1755-1769* edited by Virginia Wills (HMSO, 1973).

17.8 By his will, a Mr James Dick set up a trust for the maintenance and assistance of the parochial (not burgh) schoolmasters in the counties of Aberdeen, Banff and Moray. If your ancestor was a teacher in these counties after 1832, look in the inventory of the Dick Bequest Trust records (GD.1/4).

17.9 In terms of the Highlands Schools Act, 1838, the Treasury had to provide funds for additional schools in the Highlands. If your ancestor was a Highland schoolmaster between 1840 and 1863, look at the volumes referenced E.224/32-40. The entry 'Schools, Schedule of Grants to' in the index to each volume will lead you to the list of schoolmasters who benefited from this fund.

17.10   In 1847, the Educational Institute of Scotland, a professional association for teachers, was formed. Its records, which contain the names of many teachers who joined its ranks, also include the records of earlier mutual benefit societies formed by teachers in Glasgow (1794-1836), Roxburgh (1811-1840) and Jedburgh (1824-1872). Look at the inventory of the Institute's records (GD.342).

17.11   The Department of Education records include two volumes of reports by school inspectors before 1872. These are for the years 1859 (ED.16/13) and 1866-1867 (ED.16/14). Each volume reports on only a selection of schools, but they are indexed. Each report names the teacher and pupil-teachers of that school. Occasionally, an assistant teacher is named.

Schoolmasters since 1872

17.12   From 1872, school boards administered education at a parish level and records of the appointment of teachers and pupil-teachers are in the minute books of these school boards. School board records are mostly preserved among the records of their county council. The county council records presently held by the SRO which include school board records are those of Midlothian (CO.2/105-129), East Lothian (CO.7/5/2) and Dumfries-shire (Mouswald only, CO.9/2/1). The East Lothian records also include school log books which mention teachers (CO.7/5/4). There are a few school board minutes elsewhere in the SRO-Barra (SC.29/75/3), Dervaig (SC.59/15/4), Kilninian and Kilmore (SC.59/15/1-3), North Berwick (B.56/14), Prestonkirk (B.18/18/12) and Stornoway (SC.33/60). For other school board records, you should enquire at the relevant local record office or library.

17.13   The records of the Scottish Education Department include school inspection reports (ED.16-18). Of these, the most useful are referenced ED.16/1-12, as, although they report on only a limited number of schools between 1896 and 1909, the reports supply the names of the teachers and pupil-teachers at these schools. Some volumes include an index of schools. ED.17 and ED.18 have the advantage that there is a separate file for each school, clearly stated in the ED repertory with separate reference number, but the disadvantage that teachers are often not named or named just by their surname (eg 'Mr Cormack'). There is a 50-year closure on these records.

School Pupils and Students

17.14   Records of school pupils are rare. Some happen to be noted in school log books. As mentioned above, pupil-teachers (who existed between 1846 and 1906 and had to be at least 13 years old) are named in school board records and inspection reports. Leaving certificate registers, which give particulars of every school candidate, exist from 1908 (ED.36), but are closed for 75 years.

17.15 The records of George Heriot s School, Edinburgh, are held by the SRO and include admission registers of its boy pupils, 1659-1939 (GD.421, section 10). The SRO also has the records of Dr Guthrie's Schools (see 26.13).

17.16 Information about students of further education is best sought from the university or college they attended. Check printed sources first, as some lists of students are published. The SRO holds records of one such institution, the Edinburgh School (later College) of Art. These records include lists of applicants and students in the years 1828-1830 and 1848-1863. Look up the repertory reference NG.2/1. The lists of applicants for admission give the name, age (which could be as young as 12), profession and address of the applicant; and the lists of students, in addition to that information, give the name of the student's father.

Professors

17.17 Information about university staff is again best sought from that university. However, the appointments of some professors will be found in the Privy Seal records – look at the index to the Privy Seal English Record, 1660-1898 (PS.3) – and also in the Exchequer records described in 14.3.

$\mathcal{D}$octors and Nurses

Doctors

18.1 Since 1858, all medical practitioners in the United Kingdom have had to be registered. The SRO holds the original register of doctors in Scotland (GMC.1/2), which you are welcome to consult, but the information therein is more easily obtained from *The Medical Register* which is published annually and may be consulted in large public libraries. This publication names all registered doctors alphabetically, along with their addresses and qualifications. Remember that some doctors who registered in 1858 had been practising for many years, including William Arrott, doctor in Arbroath, whose qualifications were 'Doctor of Medicine of the University of St Andrews 1798 and Licentiate of the Royal College of Surgeons of Edinburgh 1795'. In the early entries in GMC.1/2, some dates of death are later annotated. Another annual publication which contains fuller biographical information about medical practitioners is *The Medical Directory*. There is a separate *Medical Directory for Scotland*, 1852-1860. Scottish doctors appear in the *London and Provincial Medical Directory*, 1861-1869, and thereafter in *The Medical Directory*.

18.2 For information about physicians and surgeons who had ceased to practise by 1858, you should apply to the Royal College of Physicians of Edinburgh, the Royal College of Surgeons of Edinburgh or the Royal College of Physicians and Surgeons of Glasgow (addresses in Appendix A).

Other Medical Personnel

18.3 In the Home and Health Department records, there are registers of nurses, including those working in poorhouses, between 1885 and 1930. The reference numbers are HH.2/33-37.

18.4 There are published annual registers of chemists (from 1869), dentists (from 1879), midwives (from 1917) and nurses (from 1921). Though the SRO has a copy of the Midwives Roll for Scotland (CMB.3) and the manuscript original of the Nurses' Register (GNC.12), it is suggested that you consult the published volumes in a library.

19

$\mathcal{L}$awyers

19.1 There are two principal categories of lawyers in Scotland: advocates, who alone may plead in the supreme court, the Court of Session; and solicitors, who used to be known as writers and may also be known as law agents. Law agents who plead cases in sheriff and other inferior courts may be called procurators. Judges are usually appointed from the ranks of advocates. If your ancestor was a lawyer, first examine published sources. Judges of the Court of Session up to 1832 are described in Brunton and Haig's *Senators of the College of Justice*. Advocates are listed in *The Faculty of Advocates, 1532-1943* (Scottish Record Society). Many solicitors or writers are listed in *The Register of the Society of Writers to Her Majesty's Signet* (the Society of Writers to the Signet). The procurators in Aberdeen, who confusingly called themselves advocates, are listed in the *History of the Society of Advocates in Aberdeen* (New Spalding Club, 1912). All of these books contain genealogical information. The names of lawyers also appear in various published law lists or directories, notably the *Scottish Law List* which was previously called *Index Juridicus* and which dates from 1848.

19.2 If you have exhausted the printed sources and want to examine the records in the SRO, remember that sheriffs and other judges are appointed and paid by government and therefore you might try the records mentioned in 14.1-3. Evidence of the professional career of judges, advocates and procurators will be found in the records of the court in which they operated. The Books of Sederunt of the Court of Session (cs.1) contain copies of the appointments of the Lords of Session (ie the judges) and court officers and of the admission of advocates. The records of many sheriff courts include lists of procurators authorised to plead in that court, particularly since 1874 but in some courts since the end of the 18th century. Look in the contents list of the repertory of the sheriff court for 'Register of Procurators' or 'Roll of Law Agents' or similar title: which failing, check under the Miscellaneous section. These rolls are sometimes indexed and will usually give you the business address of the lawyer. (Some sheriff courts also keep registers of sheriff officers, who are appointed by the sheriff to enforce court decrees, but who are not lawyers.)

19.3 Many writers/solicitors are also notaries and thereby authorised to certify certain legal documents. The SRO holds the Register of Admission of Notaries (NP.2) which starts in 1563 but is not a consistent record until 1661 and, as a register, stops in 1873. The warrants of admission of notaries fill some of the early gaps (NP. 3) and replace the Register from 1873 (NP.5). If you are looking for a notary prior to 1680 look first at the chronological list in NP.3/1. This list covers the years 1577-1591, 1619-1623 and 1672. For other years before 1680 you will have to go straight to the Register (NP.2). Between 1680 and 1792, look at the partly alphabetical chronological list NP.6/1, which gives the name, designation and date of admission of each notary. Order out the NP.2 volume which includes that date. Between 1792 and 1873, you have to order out the appropriate NP.2 volume and look at the index in it. Notaries admitted between 1873 and 1903 are listed briefly in NP.6/2.

19.4 All the entries in the Register of Notaries give the name and designation of the notary. Some of the earliest entries give his place of birth and state whether he is married or unmarried. Up to 1738, his age is usually given. After that date, the name of the notary's father is sometimes given, eg 'Andrew Shand Writer in Thurso Son to Andrew Shand tennant at Innes in parish of Urquhart' was admitted as a notary public on 17 June 1742 (NP.2/24).

20

*A*rchitects and Surveyors

20.1 If you are looking for an architect before 1840, first look at *A Biographical Dictionary of British Architects 1600-1840* by Howard Colvin (3rd edition, Yale University Press, 1995). For information about a Scottish architect of any date, contact the National Monuments Record of Scotland (address in Appendix A), who may provide you with relevant references in the SRO and elsewhere. In the SRO itself, there is a source list on Art and Architecture and a partial card index of references to architects in GD collections to consult. (There is a similar card index of artists.)

Vignette on plan showing name of surveyor, 1782. (RHP.22306).
Reproduced by courtesy of Lady Dick-Lauder

20.2 The profession of surveyor did not exist in Scotland until the mid-18th century. For information about most surveyors before 1850, look at the *Dictionary of Land Surveyors and Local Cartographers of Great Britain and Ireland 1550-1850*, edited by Peter Eden (William Dawson & Sons, Folkstone). This publication is in three parts and a supplement. The Scottish entries appear mainly in the supplement. The entries in it are brief, but will show that it may be worth your while to search further.

20.3   Information in the SRO about the professional careers of surveyors and architects is largely to be found in the Register House Plans (RHP). These plans are arranged and numbered in order of accession and there are now over 80,000 of them. Descriptions of non-architectural plans up to RHP.4999 are contained in the *Descriptive List of Plans in the Scottish Record Office* volumes I to 4 (Scottish Record Office), which you should find in a library. Each volume is indexed. In the West Search Room of the SRO there is a card index of architects and surveyors of plans in the RHP series up to RHP.22597. The cards in this index give the name of the surveyor or architect and the year and reference number of each plan made by him. To find a description of that plan, look it up in the RHP inventory. To find plans numbered above RHP.22597 by particular architects and surveyors, you have to read through the many volumes of the RHP inventory. The paper catalogues of plans are currently being converted on to the Clio system which will allow you to search by place and surveyor or architect.

21

Railwaymen

21.1 The SRO holds the records of those railway companies which operated in Scotland. There used to be many railway companies which gradually amalgamated. Their records are catalogued, by railway company, in the BR repertory. In the first volume of this repertory, there is a list of the companies, giving the reference of each. For example, the records of the Glasgow and South-Western Railway Company are referenced BR/GSW. The repertory is arranged in alphabetical order of reference letters. Within the records of each company, staff records are mostly listed in section 15. Thus, the staff records of the Highland Railway Company are referenced BR/HR/15. Some staff records may be found also in section 4 (miscellaneous records).

North British railwaymen, [late 19th century]. (BR/NBR/4/315).
Reproduced by courtesy of The British Railways Board.

21.2 As a first step, if possible, look at a booklet compiled by Tom Richards, *Was Your Grandfather A Railwayman?* (Federation of Family History Societies), a directory of railway archive sources for family historians. This gives useful advice on how railway staff records were kept and lists briefly the railway staff records held by the SRO and other institutions.

21.3 Railway staff recorded in the railway staff records are those who worked for the railway companies, not those who built the railways and who worked for contractors. If your ancestor was a navvy, you are very unlikely to find a record of him as such. If your ancestor worked for a railway company, you are more likely to find a record of his service if he worked in a station than if he was an engine-driver or plate-layer. You are also more likely to find him if he worked for the North British Railway Company, because more of the NB's staff records have survived.

21.4 You have to know what railway company employed your ancestor. If you know where he lived, particularly if he lived in a rural area, you may be able to guess which company. If he lived in Dufftown, you may presume that he worked for the Great North of Scotland Railway Company. If he lived in Glasgow, it may be impossible to guess which company. To find the routes and stations of the pre-1923 railway companies, look at *British Railways: Pre-Grouping Atlas and Gazetteer* (Ian Allan Ltd). In the SRO, the Station Handbooks (BR/RCH(S)/5) also tell you which companies operated which stations .

21.5 There are various types of staff records and no great consistency in compiling them. The most useful staff registers are those which give the date of birth and show the detailed career of each railwayman, from job to job and place to place. For example, BR/CAL/15/1 shows that one John Anderson (born 15 January 1866) started work for the Caledonian Railway Company as a porter at Airth in1881 and gradually moved step-by-step till he completed his career in 1924 as station-master at Guthrie on a salary of £260 per year. Other records will tell you who was employed in a particular station or department and why they ceased to be employed, either by a move to another station or department or by the end of their service. John Miller was employed by the Caledonian for 10 weeks in 1864 as a striker [metal-worker], before being discharged for smoking (BR/CAL/15/22). Offence books may tell you that your ancestor was drunk on duty or overslept and thereby delayed a train. Engine drivers were fined for not having steam up in time for their train's departure (eg in BR/GPK/4/1).

21.6 Staff records are a tiny part of the BR records but your ancestor is likely to be named in other records, such as minutes or correspondence, only if he was fairly high-up in the hierarchy or involved in an accident, eg 'David Renton, Platelayer, was run over and killed by an Engine on the Line' (1854-BR/EDP/1/5). The appointment of station masters and above are usually noted in directors' minutes (section 1), though often only the surname is given. If the minute book has an index, look under the name of the station.

21.7 Some railway records have survived in private collections, of which there are some in the GD series. These may include staff records. For instance GD.422/1/89 is a Glasgow and South Western Railway Company staff register, 1874-1922. The staff recorded in it include women, particularly some employed during the 1914-1918 war. One was Mary Brown Auld, whose service as a parcel clerk was dispensed with in 1919 'owing to a male being engaged'.

$\mathcal{C}$oal Miners

22.1 Despite their lowly status, records of the names of colliers or coal miners survive among the records of the landowner or coal company for whom they worked. In the SRO, such records are to be found among the GD collections and National Coal Board (now British Coal) records (CB) which include records of coal companies prior to nationalisation. Look first at the Coal-mining source list, which will guide you to any relevant records. None will be indexed. The Coal Board records are mainly 20th century, but do include some 18th- and 19th-century records. In them, look for wages books, pay books, oncost books and output books: the names of workers appear in records of work done by them and of payments to them.

22.2 Because the colliers are usually described simply by Christian name and surname, care is required to ensure that you have found the right man, as is evidenced by a list of colliers at Edmonstone Colliery in 1777 (GD.18/1124). The 39 colliers listed include three named Hugh Adam, three named John Archibald and several duplicated names.

22.3 Very occasionally you may find direct genealogical evidence. For example, the information 'Decr 1st 1753 Walter Simer Son to old Thomas Simer Entred Coliar' is noted in a Loanhead coal book in the Clerk of Penicuik muniments (GD.18/990/7).

22.4 Among the Stirling Sheriff Court records, there are lists of colliers in Stirlingshire who in 1799 were in debt to the proprietors of their collieries (SC.67/63/6). This is in accordance with a provision of the Colliers (Scotland) Act, 1799, which directed that debts due by colliers to their masters would cease to be valid unless they were recorded in sheriff court books within three months. There may, therefore, be such records in the records of other sheriff courts for that year.

22.5 If your ancestor met with an accident in a mine between 1861 and 1895, his name and that of the mine should be recorded in Procedure Books in the Lord Advocate's records (AD.12/19-21). Mining accidents may also feature in the sheriff court fatal accident inquiries (5.31) and workmen's compensation series (11.43).

23

Trade and Business

Burgesses, Craftsmen and Apprentices

23.1 If your ancestor was engaged in trade or business in a royal burgh, then he should appear as a burgess in the records of that burgh and possibly as a member of the guild or incorporation of his particular craft in the records of that guild or incorporation. The record of his admission as a burgess or as a member or apprentice of his craft will sometimes state a relationship. Burgesses were usually the sons or sons-in-law of burgesses. An apprenticeship commenced with an agreement (known as an indenture) between the boy's father and his master. Craftsmen admitted would usually be the sons, sons-in-law or apprentices of members of the craft.

23.2 The Scottish Record Society has published alphabetical or indexed lists of the admissions of burgesses of Edinburgh, Canongate, Glasgow and Dumbarton and of apprentices of Edinburgh. For other burghs, you will have to search the available unindexed records. Look at the repertory of burgh records (B) in the SRO to see if the records of your burgh include burgess rolls or court books which will contain the admission of burgesses. You will hope to find entries such as 'John Broun pedlar, who maried Elizabeth Mure Laufull daughter of the deceast James Mure burgess of this Burgh, in her pure Virginity,... was... Admitted Burgess and freeman of the Burgh' (Dunbar, 22 July 1730, B.18/32/7). Remember that many burgh records are not kept in the SRO but are held in the region where the burgh lies.

23.3 The SRO holds the records of the following crafts either among the burgh or Exchequer records or in the GD collections.

> Baxters (bakers) of Haddington (B.30/18/1).
> Carters in Leith (GD.399).
> Cordiners (shoemakers) of the Canongate (GD.1/14); Edinburgh
> (GD. 348); Haddington (B.30/18/2 and GD.302/62-66 and 128-129);
> Selkirk (GD.1/13).
> Dyers or Litsters of Aberdeen (E.870/4).
> Fleshers (butchers) of Ayr (E.870/6); Haddington (B.30/18/3).
> Goldsmiths of Edinburgh and Glasgow (GD.1/482).
> Hammermen (metal workers) of Burntisland (B.9/13/2); Haddington

(GD.302/130-135); Linlithgow (GD.76/390); Musselburgh (B.52/8/4-6);
Perth (GD.1/427).
Skinners of Haddington (GD.1/39/3/1).
Tailors of Edinburgh (GD.1/12); Linlithgow (GD.76/385-391).
Weavers of Ayr (E.870/5); Burntisland (B.9/15); Haddington(B.30/18/9).
Wrights and masons of Haddington (B.30/18/4-8 and B.30/22); Leith
(GD.1/943).
Wrights of Culross (GD.1/977); Musselburgh (B.52/8/1-3).

23.4 Some craft incorporation records kept elsewhere have been listed by the
National Register of Archives (Scotland). Look in the index of NRA(S)
surveys under the names of the burgh or in the classified index under 'Guilds
and Incorporations'.

23.5 There are no such records of tradesmen who operated outwith the burghs.
However, tradesmen and craftsmen may also be named in the records of
mutual benefit societies associated with their trade and craft. The GD series
include the records of the Society of Free Fishermen of Newhaven (GD.265)
and the Ancient Fraternity of Free Gardeners of East Lothian (GD.420). The
official series of friendly society records (FS) consist largely of rules and
regulations of the societies. Only a very few include mid- 19th-century lists of
members, eg the Strathaven Weavers Friendly Society (FS.1/16/204). Such
information is not noted in the FS repertory but can be found in *Labour Records
in Scotland* by Ian MacDougall (Scottish Labour History Society). Membership
of such societies sometimes extended beyond those who were strictly of the
stated trade.

23.6 Indentures of apprenticeship, whereby a boy became bound to serve a
craftsman while he learned the craft, are noted in craft records. A few such
indentures were registered in registers of deeds (see 10.2-16). Some survive in
the GDs or similar collections, eg there is a series of indentures of Edinburgh
apprentices referenced RH.9/17/274-326. Some Edinburgh apprentices
between 1695 and 1934 are recorded in the records of George Heriot's Trust
(GD.421, section 10). Do not expect an indenture to have survived: it is a bonus
if it has done so.

23.7 From 1710, stamp duty was charged on indentures of apprenticeship. The
collection of this tax was organised from London and no separate Scottish
record seems to have been kept. Some Scottish apprentices are, however,
recorded in the Stamp Board's Apprenticeship Books, 1710-1811, which are
kept in the Public Record Office (PRO reference IR.1).

Business Records

23.8 Surviving business records may or may not include wages books or other
records which name employees. There are some business records in the GD
series. For example, those of the Carron Company (GD.58) and of Alex Cowan

& Son Ltd, papermakers in Penicuik, (GD.311) include staff records. Business books, including wages books, are also to be found among the Court of Session records (see 11-25). Look also in the National Register of Archives (Scotland) index and classified index for records of business firms.

Board of Manufactures

23.9 If your ancestor was involved in fabric manufacture or the fishing industry from 1727 into the 19th century, you might want to examine the records of the Board of Trustees for Fisheries, Manufactures and Improvements in Scotland, which was established to assist economic development. Look at the repertory referenced NG.1. Among its projects, the Board awarded premiums to producers and appointed stampmasters and other inspectors to supervise the linen industry. Thus, in 1792, there were awards of £25 to William Douglas at Dalhousie for his Silesia Linen and of £15 to Donald McLeod in Arnol Island of Lewis, for oil produced from dog fish (NG.1/42/2); while, in 1822, we are told that Thomas Faulds was growing 'mostly promising' flax on the farm of Lissens in the parish of Dalry (NG.1/42/8). The regulation of the linen industry was ended in 1823, but there are superannuation records of the former inspectors up to 1859, sometimes giving their age or date of death (NG.1/48/1).

23.10 From 1809, the responsibility for overseeing the fishing industry passed to the Fishery Board for Scotland. The names of some of the men involved in the fishing industry occur in its records, particularly the records of the local fishery offices (AF.17-36), but it may take some trawling to find a name you want. Among the surviving records of fishery vessels are a few registers of establishment for the fishery cruisers the *Brenda* and the *Minna*, which include information about place and date of birth and service records of the crew, c.1898-1954 (AF.6/65-8).

Licensees

23.11 From 1756, a person who sold ale or other exciseable liquors, whether in an inn or a shop, was required to have a licence. If he operated within a burgh, then the licence was granted by the burgh court, and, if outwith a burgh, by the Justices of Peace for the county. Look in the B or JP repertory at the contents list of the relevant burgh or county for the licensing court records. Some such records are kept in local archives. Most of the surviving records start in the 19th century. We find, for example, that Mrs Isabella Laing, shipbuilder, was licensed in 1829 to sell ale in a house at the Shore of Dunbar (B.18/12/1).

$\mathscr{E}$lectors and Elected

Electors until 1832

24.1 Before 1832 only a tiny minority of Scotsmen (no women) elected representatives to Parliament, and the records of such elections are unlikely to add to the information you have about your ancestors. Representatives of the burghs were elected by the burgh council or by delegates of the councils: information is in the council minute books (B repertory). Representatives of the counties were elected by freeholders, who were men who owned land or other heritable property in that county above a certain substantial value. The records of admission of landowners on to a roll of freeholders and of the election by the freeholders of a member of parliament are to be found among the sheriff court records. Look in the contents list of an appropriate SC repertory to see if it contains the freeholders records for that county. However, as, before a man was admitted to a roll of freeholders, the instrument of sasine which proved his ownership of sufficient land had to be recorded in the Register of Sasines (see 8.3-15), the freeholders records may add nothing to what you have already found in that register. There may be points of interest where the admission or vote of a freeholder was disputed by his political opponents.

Electors since 1832

24.2 Since 1832, various Reform Acts have gradually expanded the electorate. By 1929, almost everyone over 21 was on the electoral register. Until 1918, parliamentary electors had to be male and proprietors or tenants of lands, houses or other heritable property or (since 1868) prosperous lodgers. *Electoral Registers Since 1832* by Jeremy Gibson and Colin Rogers (Federation of Family History Societies), though written from an English point of view, is useful in describing the background of electoral law. Its list of Scottish records is incomplete.

24.3 Until 1918, electoral registers had to record why an elector had the right to vote. Thus, they provide not only the name of the voter, but also his occupation, whether he is a proprietor or tenant, and a description of his property.

24.4 From 1882, provided they were proprietors or tenants, unmarried women and married women not living in family with their husband could vote for burgh councillors and, from 1889, for county councillors. From these dates, there are supplementary registers of female voters for use in local government elections.

Excerpt from Register of Voters in North Berwick, 1838. (B.56/12/2)

24.5 Registers of voters survive intermittently. Those in the SRO are almost entirely 19th century, when burghs were in separate constituencies from the counties that surrounded them. Therefore there are separate registers of voters in burghs and counties, though some registers of burgh voters survive among sheriff court records. Most burghs were grouped together, so that several burghs (sometimes in different counties) were combined to form one constituency. County registers are arranged by parishes. There are the following registers of voters in the burgh and sheriff court records in the SRO. Check the relevant repertory to obtain the exact reference.

> Burghs. Culross, 1832-1851 (B.12/7). Dunbar, 1832-1860 (B18/18). Dunfermline, 1868 (SC.67/61). Earlsferry, 1902-1904 (SC.20/46). Falkirk, 1840-1865 (SC.67/61). Hamilton, 1864-1865 (SC.67/61). Lauder, 1832-1861 (B.46/9). Newburgh, 1833-1870 (B.54/9). Newport, 1899-1900 (SC.20/46). North Berwick, 1832-1915 (B.56/12). Perth, 1876-1877 and 1892-1893 (SC.49/58). Stirling, 1868 (SC.67/61).

> Counties. Caithness, 1832-1860 (SC.14/64). Clackmannan and Kinross, 1832-1862 (SC.64/63/26-36). Cromarty, 1832-1833 (SC.24/21). Inverness, 1832-1872 (SC.29/71). Kirkcudbright, 1832-1862 (SC.16/68). Linlithgow, 1837 (SC.41/99). Nairn, 1847-1873 (SC.31/60). Peebles, 1832-1861 (SC.42/44). Roxburgh, Hawick district, 1832-1846 (SC.62/73). Selkirk, 1832-1861 (SC.63/61). Stirling, 1832-1862 (SC.67/61). Wigtown, 1832-1861 (SC.19/64).

24.6 Some of these sheriff court records also include poll books and other records of voters. Similar records may occasionally be found in GD collections, most notably GD.260, which includes electoral registers for the county of Dunbarton, 1873-1892 (GD.260/4/1-5). Enquiries about records of voters should also be made to local archives and libraries.

Members of Parliament

24.7 Though the records described above will sometimes mention those elected, you should use printed sources if you are searching for an ancestor who might have been a representative in Parliament. These include the following:

> *The Parliaments of Scotland: Burgh and Shire Commissioners*, edited by Margaret D Young (Scottish Academic Press, 1992-3) contains some 2,000 brief biographies, arranged in alphabetical order, of the men who represented the burghs and counties in the Scottish Parliament until 1707. It also contains an appendix, listing the constituencies alphabetically with names of the representatives of each.

> *Members of Parliament, Scotland, 1357-1882* by Joseph Foster.

> *The History of Parliament. The House of Commons.* A series of volumes covering 1715-1820 (History of Parliament Trust).

> *Who's Who of British Members of Parliament, 1832-1979* (The Harvester Press).

$\mathcal{T}$he Sick and Insane

The Sick

25.1 Records of patients in hospitals often supply the patient's age and sometimes date of death. Hospital records are largely in the custody of the archivist of the Health Board within whose authority the hospital lies (see addresses in Appendix A). Such records formerly in the SRO have been transmitted to the relevant Health Boards, except for a series of registers of out-patients of Dundee Royal Infirmary, 1851-1854, (cs.96/2279-2304) and the records of the Kelso Dispensary and Cottage Hospital (HH.71). Its records include lists of patients in the hospital, since 1777, supplying the patient's name, parish, age, date of admission, disease, and the outcome (mostly 'cured'). Thus, we learn that Margaret Cummins, resident in the parish of Eccles, aged 60, poisoned with laudanum, was admitted on 10 January 1828, was pumped out but died (HH.71/44). There are also some records of out-patients and patients visited at home.

25.2 Those prevented by illness from earning a living might have received poor relief (see 26.1-11). For example, in 1727, the parish of Inveravon supported 'John Fleeming a poor boy lyable to an epilepsie' (CH.2/191/2, p.244).

Lunatics

25.3 The words 'lunatic' and 'insane' are used here to describe people suffering various grades of mental disturbance. Even the best of families occasionally produce someone who is deemed not quite right in the head. Records of that person may survive if someone is appointed to administer his property or if he is put in the custody of an asylum or individual.

25.4 Obviously, only when the insane person owned property was there a need to go to law to decide who should be curator to administer that property. Until 1897, such decisions might be 'retoured to Chancery' in the same procedure as heirs were proved. This is explained in 7.4-21. Up to 1700, these decisions are to be found in the 'Inquisitiones de Tutela' in volume 2 of the *Inquisitionum Retornatarum Abbreviatio* (indexed in volume 3). After 1700, look in the 'Index to Tutories and Curatories in Record of Retours, 1701-1897'. The people indexed therein include insane persons, identifiable by being given a curator, not a tutor. To see the retour, order out by c.22 and the volume number given in the index. The curator was usually the nearest male relative on the father's side aged at least 25 years.

25.5 The retour will tell you which sheriff court held the preceding inquiry. Where records of these inquiries survive, they may provide more details both of the condition of the insane person and of his relationship to his curator. Look in the relevant SC repertory for 'Record of Services' or similar heading. For example, in 1830, James Mitchell, teacher, Kineff, was appointed curator to administer the affairs of William Gordon, bookseller, Aberdeen, his maternal uncle (C.22/133, f.89). The related Aberdeen Sheriff Court records (SC.1/27/20) supply the date of James's baptism and the names of his parents and William's father.

25.6 In the 18th century, an alternative procedure developed whereby a near relative petitioned the Court of Session for the judicial appointment of a 'curator bonis' to look after the affairs of an insane or otherwise incapable person. The records of such cases are among the records of the Court of Session (see 11.8–23).

25.7 After 1880, when the estate of an incapable person did not exceed £100 in yearly value, the appointment of a curator bonis could also be made by a sheriff court. A few sheriff courts kept a separate record of these appointments (perhaps in a 'Register of Judicial Factors'), but mostly they have to be sought among the ordinary court records (see 11.36–40).

25.8 From 1849, the Accountant of Court (of Session) was responsible for supervising curators appointed to administer the estates of persons unable to administer their own affairs. Therefore, the Accountant of Court's records include information about better-off lunatics, including cases where the curator bonis had been appointed before 1849. Look at CS.313–317 in the Court of Session repertory.

25.9 Many lunatics, of all social grades but the majority paupers, were kept in asylums. There are few records of such asylums prior to 1858. Among the Aberdeen Sheriff Court records, there are registers of lunatics in asylums in Aberdeenshire between 1800 and 1823 and between 1855 and 1857 (SC.1/18/1–2).

25.10 From 1857, such asylums were regulated by the General Board of Commissioners in Lunacy. The Board's records are preserved in the SRO, listed in the Mental Welfare Commission (MC) repertory, but are closed for 75 years. Their records include a general register of all lunatics in asylums (MC.7). This lists and numbers the inmates chronologically, from number 1, Jean Morris, who was admitted to Newbigging House in 1805 (where she died 60 years later) to number 218,009 in 1962. Though this register apparently starts in 1805, it only records those who were still alive in 1858 or were committed since 1858. The register records name, date of admission, which asylum, date of death or discharge, and whither removed (if relevant). A general index of the lunatics in the register is found at MC.7/33.

25.11 Fuller details about those admitted to asylums since 1858 are contained in the Notices of Admission (MC.2) which are arranged chronologically. The lunatic's number in the general register (MC.7) is noted on his notice of admission. Information supplied, as well as the mental and physical health of the patient, includes his full name, age, marital status, previous place of abode, nearest relative, and whether any member of his family had been insane. We find that Robert Primrose Paterson, aged 29, single, schoolmaster at Duddingstone, whose insanity was supposedly caused by 'Studying Some Educational Scheme', was admitted to the Royal Edinburgh Asylum on the petition of his mother in January 1858 (MC.2/1).

25.12 There is no register of lunatics who were not put into asylums, though they may be named in the records of poor relief (see 26.1-11). However, in the Lord Advocate's papers, there is a 'Return of lunatics or idiots at large in the county of Edinburgh [Midlothian]' in 1850 (AD.58/114). This provides the name and age of each lunatic, with whom he resides and by whom supported.

25.13 Some people accused of a crime are found to be insane. The Home and Health Department records include case books, dating from 1846, and later files on criminal lunatics (HH.17, 18 and 21/48). These are closed for 75 years.

The Poor

26.1 The poor are always with us and provision has to be made for their maintenance. In Scotland, this provision was until recently organised and recorded on a parish basis, both before and after 1845 when the system of provision was altered by the Poor Law (Scotland) Act.

26.2 Those entitled to relief from the parish were those who lacked funds or family support and were unable, through age or infirmity, to maintain themselves: poor persons who were over 70 or disabled or insane, or orphans and destitute children under 14. The able-bodied unemployed were not entitled to relief, though there might be help for their children. The parish was bound to support the infirm poor born within its bounds or resident there for five years. A married woman took her husband's parish. However, parishes did sometimes give help to an indigent visitor, usually unnamed in the records – 'a stranger', 'a poor man at the church door'; just as in practice they might help a healthy parishioner who had fallen on hard times. A parish might also provide for a non-native resident and reclaim the money from the parish of his birth. If you have an ancestor who was thus dependent on the parish, he should be named in the parish poor relief records, but you have to know to which parish he belonged, and find if and where its records have survived.

Poor Relief until 1845

26.3 Prior to the Poor Law Act, 1845, the responsibility for poor relief lay jointly with the heritors (see 8.41) and kirk session of each parish, and records of payments to the poor may be found in the records of either. Look in the indexes of parishes in both HR and CH.2 repertories and then the relevant list of records for the particular parish. Poor relief accounts were occasionally kept as a separate record and as such will be specified in the HR or CH.2 repertory. For example, the heritors of Tranent kept a very detailed poor roll between 1827 and 1845, giving details such as '79, infirm, son silly' and, of a widow, '33, young children' (HR.74/15/3). Much more commonly, payments to the poor are noted, in the midst of other business, in the minute books and account books kept by the heritors and kirk sessions. There is no short cut to searching them.

26.4 The income came from assessments on the heritors and collections at the church services. This 'poor money' was distributed to the 'Ordinary Poor' or 'Pensioners', who were paid at regular intervals and often appear in a list, and the 'Occasional Poor'. The latter category included payments in kind, such as supplying shoes or coal to a needy person; payments to the temporarily disabled, eg 10 shillings 'to one James Simpson who had his thigh bone broken' (Glencorse Kirk Session, 17 October 1700 - CH.2/181/1); and payments to those who did not belong to the parish.

26.5 Though all infirm poor within the parish, whatever their denomination, were the responsibility of the established kirk session, the free churches also sometimes assisted their own poor. However, the names of their poor people are only occasionally reported in their records (CH.3 and CH.10-16). The burgh councils also made charitable payments to people in distress, but the burgh records in the SRO (B repertory) are not very informative on this score. However, some of the burgh records which are kept in their own locality, particularly those of Edinburgh and Glasgow, are worth investigating.

Poor Relief from 1845

26.6 The Poor Law Act, 1845, established parochial boards to administer poor relief in each parish. Although the heritors and kirk sessions were no longer legally responsible for the welfare of the poor, you should still look in their records for your indigent ancestors. Most kirk sessions continued for a time to provide for their poor from church collections, eg Greenlaw distributed to named poor after the communion service twice yearly until 1881 (CH.2/183/2). Most of the members of the rural parochial boards were heritors. In some parishes they combined these functions and their heritors records continue to deal with the business of the poor. The Dirleton heritors kept a roll of poor from 1825 through to 1847, without a sign of change (HR.42/4). The parochial board business in the HR series may or may not be recorded separately from the heritors' business.

26.7 The Heritors Records (HR) are one place to look for parochial board records. Otherwise, parochial board records and records of the parish councils which replaced the boards in 1894 are preserved among the records of county councils, district councils and larger burghs, which are mostly in local archives. Apart from those in the HR series, the SRO has parochial board and parish council records of some parishes in the counties of East Lothian (CO.7/7, DC.4/4-12, DC.5/4-5, DC.7/4), Midlothian (CO.2/77-91) and Wigtownshire (CO.4/30-47). Eventually, these are all likely to be moved to an appropriate local archive.

26.8 From the genealogical point of view, it is an advantage to have an ancestor who was a pauper after 1845, as the parochial board and parish council records give full details of the people who were aided. These records are particularly useful in recording the children of aged paupers and the parentage of orphans and illegitimate and deserted children. They can also be useful in showing the

Entry from Glasserton parish poor roll, 1865. (CO.4/30/7)

geographical movements of an individual. Each parochial board had to keep a roll of poor persons to whom it gave financial relief. Among the information recorded about each pauper was age, country and place of birth, whether married or single, name and age of wife and children living with the pauper, and name and age of husband or wife and children not living in family with the pauper. Thus, we find from the register of poor of Inch parish in Wigtownshire, that Sarah Ann Hawthorne or Caldwell, a washerwoman, who declined to go into the poorhouse in 1891, was 72, born in Ireland, and had 9 children, 5 of whom were in America (CO.4/32/7, p.408).

26.9 Not everyone who applied for poor relief was added to the poor roll. Information about the applications for poor relief can be found in the parochial board minutes. Some boards also kept a separate record of applications. In 1852, the parochial board of Inch 'took up the case of Mrs Jean Finlay. The Board agree to pay the passage of her four children from Liverpool to America' (CO.4/32/1), although there was no provision in the Poor Law (Scotland) Act for assisting emigration.

26.10 An applicant who was refused relief by the inspector of poor for a parish could appeal to the sheriff of the sheriffdom in which that parish lay. An inspector of poor could apply to the sheriff for the removal from the country of a pauper who was not a native of Scotland, and also could raise an action in the sheriff court against a father who had deserted his wife and children or refused to support an illegitimate child. The sheriff court records (SC) therefore contain records of such cases.

26.11 A few sheriff courts kept separate records of applications for poor relief: Ayr, 1846-1933 (SC.6/82); Banff, 1890-1910 (SC.2/7); Elgin, 1846-1851 (SC.26/66/1); and Hamilton, 1848-1865 (SC.37/18/8). Apart from those, the records of cases relating to poor relief have to be sought among the records of other Ordinary Court cases brought before the sheriff (see 11.36-40). Identifying them may not be easy and the detail given may be minimal. If there is a register of summary applications, look there. Glasgow Sheriff Court's register (SC.36/7) is particularly useful, as it starts in 1858, earlier than most. In such a register, look under 'Pursuer or Applicant' for a person appealing against refusal of relief and under 'Respondent' for a person who was to be removed to Ireland or England or had deserted wife and children.

Destitution

26.12 The parish system of poor relief sometimes proved insufficient and had to be supplemented by private charity. To find the records of charitable foundations, sometimes called 'hospitals', which helped the poor of particular localities, you should first check the regional or district archive which serves that locality. The records of the King James VI Hospital, Perth, are in the SRO. Look in the GD.79 inventory at section 7 for records of the deserving poor of Perth. In 1825, an application was made on behalf of the Widow Macphail, in South Street, aged 102 years (GD.79/7/38/1).

26.13 In the cities, charitable institutions were established for the maintenance and education of orphans and other destitute children. Two such institutions of which the records are held by the SRO are the Dean Orphanage (GD.417) and Dr Guthrie's Schools (GD.425), both in Edinburgh. Records which name children date from 1753 and 1854 respectively, but these records less than 100 years old are closed to the public. Petitions for admission and admission registers can provide useful family information. James Ralston, admitted to Dean Orphanage in 1830, was the son of an army sergeant. His mother 'also followed the Camp since she was 11 years of age', suffering fatigue and exposure during the Peninsular Campaigns (GD.417/175).

26.14 In response to the devastating failure of the potato crop in it 1846, destitution boards were established to raise money to save the people of the Highlands and Islands from starvation. The records of these boards, listed in the Highland Destitution (HD) repertory, name many of the people in the Highlands and Islands who between 1847 and 1852 were given meal or financial aid or were found work. Look at the registers listed as HD.1. These registers vary in content but usually supply the name, age and occupation of each head of family, sometimes also the number of children in that family, and sometimes the names and ages of everyone in the family. Thus, we find that in May 1847, Mathew Jameson, a farmer and fisherman at Ollabury in the district of Northmaven in Shetland, was 35 and had one child above 12 and four under 12 (HD.1/1). A register of the most needy families in Skye in 1850 (HD.1/13) tells us that Donald McDiarmid, at Kilmuir in the district of Watternish, was aged 60 and his family consisted of Alice (45), Norman (7) and John (4). HD.1 is not a complete series, but similar information can be found in meal distribution accounts (HD.6/9-13) and in some of the papers relating to Shetland (HD.17), Skye (HD.20) and Wester Ross (HD.21), particularly the abstracts of registry and applications for work. An equivalent record in the Tobermory Sheriff Court records is a register of meal distribution, 1848- 1853, to paupers in and around Mull (SC.59/15/5).

Children at the Orphan Hospital of Edinburgh, later
the Dean Orphanage, 18th-century. (GD 417/255/9).
Reproduced by courtesy of the Secretaries and Treasurers of
that Dean Orphanage and Cauvin's Trust.

27

$\mathscr{M}igrants$

27.1 There is ample proof that Scotsmen migrated, both within the British Isles and overseas. Yet records of the actual movement of individual migrants are sparse. Free movement within the United Kingdom has always been possible, but the evidence has to be dug out of records designed for other purposes, such as kirk session or parochial board records. There is no official record of the ordinary Scots who migrated to Northern Ireland in the reign of James VI, only of their well-to-do landlords.

27.2 There was similar freedom of travel abroad, generally unrecorded except for transported criminals (see 12.22). Passports, as we know them, were not introduced until 1915. Previously, the Crown sometimes issued passes or letters of protection to people travelling in Europe, but these people were from the upper classes and intending to return. Before 1603, some of these letters were recorded in the Register of the Privy Seal (see 5. 17). Records of later passports are mainly in the Public Record Office in London. Official ship passenger lists exist only from 1890 and these are also in the Public Record Office.

27.3 If your ancestor emigrated to North America or Australia, look for him in the immigration records in the country of arrival or in the various published lists which are available such as:

> *Passenger and Immigration Lists Index - A Guide to Published Arrival Records of about 500,000 Passengers in the United States and Canada* by P William Filby and Mary K Meyer (Gale Research Company, Detroit).

> *Directory of Scottish Settlers in North America, 1625-1825*, 6 volumes, by David Dobson (Genealogical Publishing Company, Baltimore).

> *A Dictionary of Scottish Emigrants to the USA*, 2 volumes, by Donald Whyte (Magna Carta Book Company, Baltimore).

> *A Dictionary of Scottish Emigrants to Canada Before Confederation* by Donald Whyte (Ontario Genealogical Society).

27.4 There are, however, two bodies of records in the SRO which deal specifically with short-lived 19th-century schemes to assist emigrants from the western Highlands and Islands.

27.5 The Highland and Island Emigration Society was a voluntary association formed in 1851. Its records are referenced HD.4. They include lists of assisted emigrants who sailed to Australia between 1852 and 1857 (HD.4/5). The emigrants are listed by ship and by family, giving the name and age of each person and where they had resided in western Scotland.

27.6 Files concerning a later scheme for state-aided emigration to Canada are listed in the AF repertory under AF.51. Files which provide family details of those who applied to emigrate are dated between 1886 and 1889. They include lists of applicants from some of the Western Isles and completed forms of application for assistance to emigrate. These record the members of the household of the applicant, stating each's age and relationship to the applicant. If any failed to embark, this is noted. Thus, we know that William Macleod (26), from Coll, emigrated with his wife and brother, but his cousin Donald MacDonald changed his mind and stayed behind (AF.51/36). Some information about emigrants in Manitoba after 1889 is contained in the records of the Crofters and Cottars Colonization Board (AF.51/188–211).

28

Genealogies

28.1 Ancestor-hunting or the pursuit of pedigree is not a new endeavour. Published genealogies of Scottish families are listed in *Scottish Family History* by Margaret Stuart and Balfour Paul and *Scottish Family Histories* by J P S Ferguson. Manuscript genealogies of varying antiquity may be found in archives and libraries, such as those of the Scottish Genealogy Society and the Lyon Office (addresses in Appendix A).

28.2 Unless you are of the aristocracy or landed gentry, you will not find your own family tree ready-made. Nevertheless, having laboured to find some ancestors, there is always an outside chance that you might honestly graft your family tree on to one that someone has already compiled; a greater chance if you find a well-born ancestor. Be canny, though. Not every genealogy may be totally accurate. Check the details, if you can.

28.3 There are some genealogies among the manuscripts in the SRO. RH.16 is a collection of genealogies, indexed at the end of the RH.16 inventory. Otherwise, seek for genealogies in the GD collections. Look in the GD.1 card index for ones in the GD.1 series. A few of the GDs consist of papers gathered and compiled by people who did research. From our point of view, the most useful of these is The John MacGregor Collection (GD.50) which, along with original papers and transcripts of documents, contains genealogies and genealogical notes, mainly of Highland families, especially MacGregors and Campbells. As the GD.50 inventory is arranged in no logical order, you should examine it carefully. Some GD collections of the records of landed and noble families include genealogies and family narratives, usually but not exclusively of their own and related families. These genealogies may or may not be evident in the inventory contents list: try the miscellaneous section, if there is one.

28.4 Let us take as our final words on the ancestors we seek a quotation which appears at the foot of a pedigree of the family of Hays of Rannes and Lenplum in the Rose of Montcoffer papers (GD.36/273).

> *'Blessed are the Dead which die in the Lord . . .*
> *that they may rest from their Labours,*
> *and their Works do follow them.'*
> Revelations, xiv, 13

APPENDIX A

*U*seful Addresses

NATIONAL INSTITUTIONS

Scottish Record Office
HM General Register House
Edinburgh
EH1 3YY
Phone: 0131-535 1314

National Register of Archives (Scotland)
West Register House
Charlotte Square
Edinburgh
EH2 4DF
Phone: 0131-535 1314

General Register Office for Scotland
New Register House
Edinburgh
EH1 3YT
Phone: 0131-334 0380
      0131 -314 4433

Court of the Lord Lyon
New Register House
Edinburgh
EH1 3YT
Phone: 0131-556 7255

National Library of Scotland
George IV Bridge
Edinburgh
EH1 1EW
Phone: 0131-226 4531

National Monuments Record of
  Scotland
Royal Commission on the Ancient and
  Historical Monuments of Scotland
16 Bernard Terrace
Edinburgh EH8 9NX
Phone: 0131-662 1456

Scottish United Services Museum
The Castle
Edinburgh
EH1 2NG
Phone: 0131-225 7534

Scottish Catholic Archives
16 Drummond Place
Edinburgh
EH3 6PL
Phone: 0131-556 3661

LOCAL ARCHIVES

Aberdeen City Archives
Old Aberdeen House
Dunbar Street
Aberdeen
AB24 1UF
Phone: 01224 481775

Aberdeen City Archives
Town House
Aberdeen
AB9 1AQ
Phone: 01224 276276

Argyll and Bute Archives
Kilmory
Lochgilphead
Argyll
PA31 8RT
Phone: 01546 604120

Dumfries Archive Centre
33 Burns Street
Dumfries
DG1 2PS
Phone: 01387 269254

Dumfries and Galloway Library Service
Ewart Public Library
Catherine Street
Dumfries
DG1 1JB
Phone: 01387 253820

City of Dundee Archive and Record Centre
City Chambers
City Square
Dundee
DD1 3BY
Phone: 01382 223141

Edinburgh City Archives
City Chambers
High Street
Edinburgh
EH1 1YJ
Phone: 0131-529 4616

Edinburgh Room
Edinburgh City Libraries
George IV Bridge
Edinburgh
EH1 1EG
Phone: 0131-225 5584

Glasgow City Archives
Mitchell Library
North Street
Glasgow
G3 7DN
Phone: 0141-287 2910

Highland Council Archive Services
Inverness Library
Farraline Park
Inverness
IV1 1NH
Phone: 01463 220330

The History Research Centre
Callendar House
Callendar Park
Falkirk
FK1 1YR
Phone: 01324 503 778/9

Midlothian Council Archives
Library Headquarters
2 Clark Street
Loanhead
EH20 9DR
Phone: 0131-440 2210 ext. 226

The Mitchell Library
Rare Books and Manuscripts Department
North Street
Glasgow
G3 7DN
Phone: 0141-221 7030

The Moray Record Office
The Tolbooth
High Street
Forres
IV36 0AB
Phone: 01309 673617

North Highland Archives
Carnegie Library
Sinclair Terrace
Wick
KW1 5AB
Phone: 01955 606432

North Lanarkshire Archives
Airdrie Library
Wellwynd
Airdrie
ML6 OA9
Phone: 01236 763 221

Orkney Archives
The Orkney Library
Laing Street
Kirkwall
KW15 1NW
Phone: 01856 3166

Perth and Kinross District Archive
AK Bell Library
York Place
Perth
PH2 8EP
Phone: 01738 447 022

Scottish Borders Archive and
  Local History Centre
St Mary's Mill
Selkirk
TD7 3EU
Phone: 01750 20842

Shetland Archives
44 King Harald Street
Lerwick
ZE1 0EQ
Phone: 01595 3535

Stirling Council Archives
Unit 6
Burghmuir Industrial Estate
Stirling
FK7 7PY
Phone: 01786 450745

West Lothian Council
Records Management Unit
7 Rutherford Square
Brucefield Industrial Estate
Livingston
EH54 9BU
Phone: 01506 460 020

UNIVERSITIES

Aberdeen University Library
Department of Special Collections and Archives
King's College
Aberdeen
AB9 2UB
Phone: 01224 272599

Dundee University Library
Archives and Manuscripts Department
The University
Dundee
DD1 4HN
Phone: 01382 23181

Edinburgh University Library
Special Collections Departments
George Square
Edinburgh
EH8 9LJ
Phone: 0131-667 1011

Glasgow University Archives
The University
Glasgow
G12 8QQ
Phone: 0141-330 5516

Heriot-Watt University Archives
Riccarton.
Currie
Edinburgh
EH14 4AS
Phone: 0131-449 5111

St Andrews University Library
Department of Manuscripts
North Street
St Andrews
KY16 9TR
Phone: 01334 76161

Strathclyde University Archives
University of Strathclyde
McCance Building
16 Richmond Street
Glasgow
G1 1XQ
Phone: 0141-552 4400

MEDICAL RECORDS

Greater Glasgow Health Board Archive
University of Glasgow
Glasgow
G12 8QQ
Phone: 0141-330 5516

Lothian Health Board
Medical Archives Centre
Edinburgh University Library
George Square
Edinburgh
EH8 9LJ
Phone: 0131-650 3392

Northern Health Services Archives
ARI Woolmanhill
Aberdeen
AB1 1LD
Phone: 01224 663 456 ext. 55562
or 01224 663 123

Royal College of Physicians of Edinburgh
9 Queen Street
Edinburgh
EH2 1JQ
Phone: 0131-225 7324

Royal College of Physicians and Surgeons of
 Glasgow
234-242 St Vincent Street
Glasgow
G2 5RS
Phone: 0141-221 6072

Royal College of Surgeons of Edinburgh
18 Nicolson Street
Edinburgh
EH8 9DW
Phone: 0131-556 6206

ASSOCIATIONS

Aberdeen and North-East Family History
 Society
152 King Street
Aberdeen
AB2 3BD
Phone: 01224 646323

Association of Scottish Genealogists and
 Record Agents
PO Box No 174
Edinburgh
EH3 5QZ

Scots Ancestry Research Society
3 Albany Street
Edinburgh
EH1 3PY
Phone: 0131-556 4220

Scottish Genealogy Society
15 Victoria Terrace
Edinburgh
EH1 2JL

Scottish Record Society
Secretary: Dr James Kirk
Department of Scottish History
University of Glasgow
G12 8QQ

Tay Valley Family History Society
179 Princes Street
Dundee
DD4 6DQ

ENGLAND

Public Record Office
Ruskin Avenue
Kew
Richmond
TW9 4DU
Phone: 0181–876 3444

IRELAND

Public Record Office of Northern Ireland
66 Balmoral Avenue
Belfast
BT9 6NY
Phone: 01232 661 6210

The National Archives
Four Courts
Dublin 1
Republic of Ireland
Phone: 01 7338 33

$\mathcal{U}$seful Books

Various published works are recommended at appropriate points in the text. The following list repeats some of the more useful of them and also suggests further publications which you may wish to consult. The names of publishers arc placed in brackets.

Annual Report of the Keeper of the Records of Scotland (Copies may be purchased from the Scottish Record Office. Microfiche copies of the Reports from 1979 onwards may be purchased from Chadwyck-Healey Ltd, The Quorum, Bramwell Road, Cambridge CD5 8FW.)

The Concise Scots Dictionary (Aberdeen University Press)

In Search of Scottish Ancestry by Gerald Hamilton-Edwards (Phillimore)

Index of Scottish Place Names from 1971 Census (Her Majesty's Stationery Office)

The New Statistical Account of Scotland (15 volumes, published 1845)

Scotland. A Genealogical Research Guide (The Genealogical Library, Salt Lake City)

Scottish Family History by Margaret Stuart and Sir James Balfour Paul (Oliver & Boyd; reprinted by Genealogical Publishing Company, Baltimore)

Scottish Family Histories by Joan P S Ferguson (National Library of Scotland)

Scottish Family History by David Moody (Batsford)

The Scottish Genealogist, the quarterly journal of the Scottish Genealogy Society (address in Appendix A)

Sources for Scottish Genealogy and Family History by D J Steel (Phillimore, for Society of Genealogists)

Scottish Roots by Alwyn James (Macdonald Publishers)

The Statistical Account of Scotland compiled by Sir John Sinclair (21 volumes, published 1791-1799; reprinted by E P Publishing)

The Surnames of Scotland by George F Black (The New York Public Library)

Tracing Your Ancestors in the Public Record Office by Jane Cox and Timothy Padfield (The Stationery Office)

Tracing your Ancestors in Northern Ireland by Ian Maxwell, edited by Grace McGrath (The Stationery Office)

Wills and Where to Find Them by J W S Gibson (Phillimore)

A list of Scottish Record Office publications and other items for sale at the SRO will be sent on request.

Many useful calendars and indices of Scottish records have been and are being published by the Scottish Record Society. The Secretary's address is in Appendix A. The Society's earlier publications are unfortunately out-of-print.

Index of Classes and Types of Records

Index of Categories of Individuals

Published by The Stationery Office Limited and available from:

The Stationery Office Bookshops
71 Lothian Road. Edinburgh EH3 9AZ
(counter service only)
59-60 Holborn Viaduct, London EC1A 2FD
(Temporary Location until Mid-1998)
Fax 0171-831 1326
68-69 Bull Street, Birmingham B4 6AD
0121-236 9696 Fax 0121-236 9699
33 Wine Street, Bristol BSI 2BQ
0117-926 4306 Fax 0117-929 4515
9-21 Princess Street, Manchester M60 8AS
0161-834 7201 Fax 0161-833 0634
16 Arthur Street, Belfast BT1 4GD
01232 238451 Fax 01232 235401
The Stationery Office Oriel Bookshop
The Friary, Cardiff CFI 4AA
01222 395548 Fax 01222 384347

The Stationery Office publications are also available from:

The Publications Centre
(mail, telephone and fax orders only)
PO Box 276, London SW8 5DT
General enquiries 0171-873 0011
Telephone orders 0171-873 9090
Fax orders 0171-873 8200

Accredited Agents
(see Yellow Pages)

and through good booksellers

Printed in Scotland for The Stationery Office Limited
J30024, C100, 11/97, CCN003808